Annabel Karmel's

complete family

meal planner

Annabel Karmel's

complete family

meal planner

over 150 wonderfully easy and healthy recipes for all
the family from the best-selling author of
THE NEW COMPLETE BABY AND TODDLER MEAL PLANNER

EBURY
PRESS

**For my children Nicholas, Lara and Scarlett,
a constant source of inspiration**

First published as *Family Meal Planner* in 1999; revised and updated as *Favourite Family Recipes* in 2005
This revised and updated edition published 2009

1 3 5 7 9 10 8 6 4 2

First published in 1999 by Ebury Press, an imprint of Ebury Publishing
A Random House Group Company

The Random House Group Limited Red. No. 954009

Addresses for companies within the Random House Group can be found at
www.randhomhouse.co.uk

A CIP catalogue record for this book is available from the British Library

The Random House Group Limited supports The Forest Stewardship Council (FSC), the leading international forest certification
organisation. All our titles that are printed on Greenpeace approved FSC certified paper carry the FSC logo. Our paper procurement
policy can be found at www.rbooks.co.uk/environment

To buy books by your favourite authors and register for offers visit www.rbooks.co.uk

ISBN 978-0-09-193219-0

Project editor: Emma Callery
Designer: Alison Shackleton
Photographers: Daniel Pangbourne, except for page 7 by Harry Ormisher and page 49 by Philip Wilkins, and pages 2, 5, 18, 19, 32,
48–9, 54, 63, 70, 88, 102, 122, 123, 126, 132, 152, 155, 161, 163, 171, 174, 182 and 185 and cover, by Dave King
Home economists: Val Barrett and Dagmar Vesseley
Stylists: Tessa Evelegh and Jo Harris
Illustrations: Nadine Wickenden
Consultant nutritionist: Christine Carter Bsc SRD Specialist Paediatric Dietitian at Great Ormond Street Hospital for Sick Children

Printed and bound in China by C&C Offset

Contents

Introduction

This book will take the worry out of everyday cooking because with it alongside you, you will know that you'll always have something in the house that can be made into a tasty meal for the family. These are some of my favourite tried and tested recipes for all occasions from healthy breakfasts, through to lunchboxes, family suppers, recipes for entertaining and even fun foods for children to cook themselves. As a busy mother of three children, I know how difficult it can be to find the time to make a home-cooked meal and so I have tried to create recipes that are quick and easy to prepare, healthy and, of course, tasty. Each recipe has been tested on a panel of children who, naturally, didn't care how healthy the food was and were only impressed if it tasted good.

For many children, convenience and junk foods are no longer occasional foods but are becoming a regular part of their diet and in this age of instant gratification, fewer and fewer families are sitting down to meals together. With the proliferation of processed packaged foods, many meals emanate from the freezer to be cooked in the microwave and the kitchen is fast becoming the coldest room in the house. Healthy eating for children is crucial as it often sets the dietary pattern for life, and eating healthily from a young age can reduce the risk of developing diet-related diseases like heart disease and some forms of cancer. For fighting disease, food is still the best medicine.

Food is more than just a biological need, its preparation expresses parental love and caring and it's so very satisfying to see your family enjoy your lovingly prepared home-cooked meals. There was once a time when children ate largely the same as their parents and this book aims to provide you with recipes that the whole family will enjoy together. You don't need to be a Supercook. These recipes don't require split-second timing, special skills or expensive equipment and most of them can be prepared in less than 30 minutes.

Some weeks you'll be able to plan ahead and know what you're going to feed the family for supper on Friday when it's still only Monday, and other weeks you may only have time to think about Friday's dinner on Friday.

A bit of time spent planning, cooking ahead and freezing some meals over the weekend will make the week ahead much more manageable. Decide on the week's meals and what advance cooking you can do over the weekend. Then make a shopping list for the week and jot down on a calendar the fresh ingredients you will need to pick up during the week. Naturally there will be weekends where you're busy or the weather is too nice to spend time in the kitchen and so you can just plan simple meals for the week ahead like Teriyaki Chicken Skewers (page 73), Salad and Fresh Fruit. There will also be occasions when you haven't even had time to do the shopping and it's already six o'clock, but you don't need to panic as there are lots of ideas here for delicious recipes which can be made from basic store-cupboard ingredients.

Rather than thinking what are we going to eat and what are the children going to eat, we should be thinking of one meal for the whole family. A good solution to the problem of family members who want meals at different times of the day is to freeze some food in individual portion sizes so that you have your own stock of healthy convenience foods that can be heated up in the microwave in a matter of minutes. Very often when you are making a recipe it takes very little extra time to prepare more than you need so you have portions leftover to freeze.

International cuisine can be another source of inspiration – perhaps make a Chinese dinner for the family choosing some of the delicious easy to prepare Chinese-style recipes from the book such as Super vegetarian spring rolls followed by Chinese noodles with prawns and beansprouts and lychees with Caramelised almond ice cream for dessert. Wouldn't it be fun to eat the food with chopsticks – you can buy child friendly-plastic chopsticks that are joined at the top, which makes it very easy for children to use them.

This is a book of everyday family eating and I hope it will be well-thumbed and splattered with food and will help busy lifestyles become less chaotic. My aim is that this book will put the joy back into cooking, which is after all a labour of love.

Annabel Karmel

Organization

It's getting late, you've got work to finish for the next day, the phone keeps ringing, the children want help with their homework and you haven't even thought about what you can make for supper. Do you find yourself staring at the contents of your larder for inspiration – well, here's the answer to your problems.

First of all a list of ingredients to stock in your kitchen so that you will always be able to rustle up a delicious meal for the family and secondly lots of recipes which can be frozen ahead. It takes very little extra effort or time to cook more than you need and freeze extra portions so you always have a store of tasty, healthy recipes which can be defrosted and cooked at your convenience.

Coming up with varied meals can't always be done at the last minute. It's a good idea to work out what you will make 3 or 4 days in advance, write a list and buy all the fresh ingredients that you don't already keep in your kitchen from the supermarket. With Internet shopping you don't even need to leave home and it's a good idea to plan in advance.

Remember that it's easy to make more than you need when cooking a recipe and freeze extra portions so that you don't need to cook every day.

THE HEALTHY STORECUPBOARD

The key to making your life easier when it comes to planning weekly menus is stocking your kitchen with good basic ingredients. I have put together lists of the foods you need to try to keep in stock, basing them on the recipes in the book. Don't feel that you have to buy everything at once and you could simply choose a selection of recipes that you would like to prepare and just buy the ingredients for those recipes.

Dry foods
Bread
Rice: basmati, long-grain and brown rice
Flour: wholemeal, plain, self-raising, cornflour, strong white
Baking soda
Bicarbonate of soda
Dried yeast
Pasta: penne, tagliatelle, spaghettini, short-cut macaroni, lasagne, Chinese egg noodles
Sugar: caster sugar, light brown sugar, light muscovado sugar, icing sugar
Breakfast cereal: porridge, muesli, wheatgerm, etc.
Dried fruit: eg apricots, raisins, sultanas
Nuts: ground almonds, pecans, peanuts
Grains that don't take long to prepare, eg couscous, bulgar wheat
Split red lentils, green lentils
Desiccated coconut
Good quality plain and white chocolate
Cocoa powder
Skimmed milk powder

Tinned produce and jars
Chopped plum tomatoes
Sweetcorn
Baked beans
Coconut milk
Passata
Good quality ready-made tomato sauce
Sun-dried tomatoes
Peanut butter
Golden syrup, maple syrup, honey
Yeast extract
Sardines
Tuna fish in oil
Condensed cream of tomato soup
Condensed cream of mushroom soup
Condensed milk
Evaporated milk
Mandarin oranges
Raspberries
Peaches

Dried herbs and ground spices
Mixed dried herbs, basil, bay leaves, oregano, thyme, marjoram, paprika, turmeric, cumin, chilli powder, blades of mace, nutmeg, black peppercorns, cinnamon, curry powder, ground ginger

Fruit and vegetables
Variety of fruit
Salad vegetables
Onions

Garlic
Fresh ginger

Sauces, oils and seasonings
Olive oil, sunflower oil, vegetable oil,
sesame oil
Red wine vinegar, balsamic vinegar, rice
wine vinegar (may find in Oriental food
section of store), cider vinegar, malt
vinegar
Soy sauce
Oyster sauce
Worcestershire sauce
Tomato purée
Tomato sauce
Red pesto
Hoisin sauce
Salad cream
Mayonnaise
Honey
Maple syrup
Curry powder
Dry mustard powder
Dijon mustard
Chicken stock and vegetable stock
cubes or use jars of stock
Sesame seeds
Pure vanilla essence
Lemon juice

Alcohol
Dry white wine
Sake
Mirin
Sherry

IN THE REFRIGERATOR
To obtain the longest life possible
from perishable foods it would be a
good idea to wash and tidy your
fridge once a week.

Check its temperature: it should be
32-41°F (0-5°C) and if your fridge
is not already equipped with a
thermometer, it would be a good
idea to purchase one – many
fridges do not store food at a low
enough temperature.

Dairy and cooked foods should be
stored at the top of the fridge with
raw meats below in a sealed
container.

Butter
Soft margarine
Low-fat plain yoghurt
Cheddar cheese
Gruyère cheese
Edam cheese
Parmesan cheese
Cream cheese
Eggs
Milk
Ready-made custard

IN THE FREEZER
It's a good idea to freeze bread and
butter for emergencies. It's also
good to keep some ready-made
frozen foods like pizzas, or chicken
or fish in breadcrumbs in the
freezer.

Frozen peas
Frozen leaf spinach
Frozen sweetcorn
Frozen low-fat oven chips
Frozen pizza
Frozen chicken breasts
Fish fillets with or without
breadcrumbs
Lean minced meat
Lamb chops
Good quality dairy ice cream
Frozen raspberries

If you are buying fish or chicken
in breadcrumbs or batter, choose
larger portion sizes as there will be
less coating in proportion to the
fish or chicken.

Buy thick-cut oven chips – the
thicker they are, the less fat they
contain.

 Indicates recipes suitable for children to make.

 Indicates recipes suitable for freezing.

The Food Pyramid

Eating a balanced diet is all to do with choosing the right foods and eating them in the right proportion. For most of us that will mean eating more bread, cereals, starchy foods like potatoes, pasta and rice and more fruits and vegetables. This is the type of diet that adults and children over five should be eating.

Children under five need a diet higher in fat and lower in fibre because of their high energy requirements and, unlike their parents, they are also growing. Gradually their diet will change to become more in line with that of an adult diet, lower in fat, particularly saturated fat, and higher in fibre. It is helpful to think of food groups rather than individual foods. The foods at the bottom of the pyramid are the ones we should be eating more of and we should aim to eat less food from the food groups near the top.

Fats, oils and sweets use in moderation

Meat, poultry, fish, dry beans, eggs and nuts 2-3 servings

Milk, yoghurt and cheese 2-3 servings

Vegetables and fruits 5 servings

Bread, cereal, rice and pasta 6-11 servings

A balanced diet should contain approximately 20% protein, 35% fat, 45% carbohydrate

CARBOHYDRATES

These are the body's main source of energy and also provide vitamins, minerals and fibre. Bread, pasta, potatoes and rice can be used as the basis for many quick, healthy meals. Many people believe starchy foods like bread and potatoes are high in calories, but this is not true. Plain boiled new potatoes are not fattening but adding lots of butter to a baked potato can double its calorie content. A slice of bread contains about 65 calories but buttering it increases this to 142 calories and spreading jam on top adds another 39 calories. Of course, this is less important for children who need more fat in their diet under the age of five, unless overweight. Wholegrain cereals and breads boost your intake of iron, vitamins and fibre.

There are two types of carbohydrates: sugars and starches. In both types there are two forms again.

Sugars: natural fruits and vegetables
refined sugars and honey, soft drinks, cakes, biscuits, jam, confectionery.

Starches: *Complex carbohydrates*: wholegrain breakfast cereal, wholemeal bread and flour, brown rice, potatoes, peas, bananas and many other fruits and vegetables.
Refined carbohydrates: processed breakfast cereals, white flour, bread and pasta, white rice, biscuits and cakes.

It is the complex carbohydrates and natural sugars that should form at least 50% of the calories in your diet.

Refined carbohydrates like white bread and processed sweet breakfast cereals have lost many of their valuable nutrients during processing. Eat more complex carbohydrates, these are energy-rich foods, they keep your blood sugar level constant because they release their sugar content into the bloodstream slowly. They also retain their vitamins and minerals and contain fibre, which encourages the elimination of toxins in the body. *See Vitamins on page 15 for information on fruits and vegetables.*

PROTEIN

It is reassuring to know that protein deficiency is almost unheard of in this country and most of us eat more protein than we need. Protein is essential for growth and repair of body tissue and an inadequate supply of protein can lower resistance to disease and infection. The major protein foods are meat, chicken, fish, eggs, dairy products, beans and lentils. It is good to serve one of these foods for lunch and supper. It's also quite likely that you might serve protein foods like cheese or eggs at breakfast too. Protein should make up to 15   20% of your daily diet.

As a rough guide, eat meat or chicken 3-4 times a week, and it is recommended that two portions of fish are eaten each week, one of which should be an oily variety like mackerel, tuna, salmon or sardines. These and other oily fish are high in omega-3 fatty acids, which help lower blood pressure, and there is evidence that these fatty acids may help to protect against heart disease and strokes. Sardines are also a good source of bone-strengthening calcium and vitamin B12. *See Brain-boosting foods on page 12 on importance of essential fatty acids for brain function.*

FOODS CONTAINING FAT, FOODS CONTAINING SUGAR

Cakes, biscuits, sweets, crisps and soft drinks fall into this group. As they often contain large quantities of fat, sugar and salt, they should only be eaten occasionally and in small amounts. For adults and children over five, fat should provide no more than 35% of their total calorie intake. The way to achieve this is to cut down on junk food, cakes and biscuits. However, it's not realistic to ban these types of food altogether and they are perfectly fine as occasional foods or part of a meal.

Fats in moderation are an essential part of our diet. Fat makes food more palatable and plays an important role in providing energy, particularly in the diets of young children. It also facilitates the absorption of the fat-soluble vitamins A, D, E and K. Vegetable oils and fish provide the essential fatty acids that the body cannot manufacture from other constituents in the diet.

There are two types of fat: saturated and unsaturated. Saturated fat is derived mainly from animal sources, eg meat, butter, cheese, eggs and margarine, and unsaturated fat come from vegetable sources, eg olive oil, sunflower oil, soft polyunsaturated margarine and oily fish like mackerel. We all need a certain amount of fat in our diet but it is the type of fat that is important. Saturated fats can increase blood cholesterol levels and high intakes are linked to heart disease. It is a good idea to choose lean meats and vegetable oils for frying rather than butter. Cheese contains saturated fat; it is also a good source of calcium, protein and vitamins.

FIVE PORTIONS A DAY

Health experts recommend that we should try to include five portions of fruit and vegetables in our diet every day. This helps to protect against cancers and heart disease and provides the right balance of vitamins, minerals and fibre. As well as providing vitamins and minerals, fruit and vegetables also contain many other biologically active substances called phytochemicals. There is growing scientific evidence for the anti-cancer effects of the 500 phytochemicals identified so far and there may be thousands more.

Different fruits and vegetables contain different vitamins and minerals so try to include as much variety as you can. Fruits, vegetables and juice high in vitamin C help iron to be absorbed from other foods, so ensure you and your family eat some at each meal. Also fruit and vegetables are low in fat and calories and provide a natural source of fibre, which helps to keep the digestive system in order. Vitamin supplements contain only a small proportion of the benefits available in fruits and vegetables themselves.

BRAIN-BOOSTING FOODS

Don't let your child skip breakfast. Numerous studies have shown that a high-fibre breakfast – muesli, porridge, wholegrain cereal or toast – helps to ensure a steady supply of blood sugar for long-lasting energy and good concentration. Sugary refined cereals and white bread are broken down quickly, rapidly releasing sugar in the blood. This gives a quick burst of energy followed by a drop in sugar levels, leaving a child tired, unable to concentrate and hungry.

Iron deficiency is the most common nutritional deficiency in developed countries. Two of the main symptoms are tiredness and lack of concentration, so increasing iron intake could well improve your child's schoolwork as well as health. Iron is important for transporting oxygen in the blood to all organs in the body including the brain, therefore iron is important for good brain function. Red meat provides the best source of iron (see page 14).

Oily fish rich in omega-3 fatty acids are important for brain function and concentration, so try to give children fish like fresh tuna, salmon, sardines or mackerel twice a week or buy Columbus eggs, which are rich in fatty acids. Some hyperactive children are deficient in essential fatty acids and it is worthwhile having them tested, as research suggests that taking a 1,000 mg supplement of omega oils can help improve concentration in children who have attention defect disorders and can also help with dyspraxia.

Keeping hydrated helps the brain function at its best so make sure your child drinks plenty of water. Children need about 1.25 litres (2 pints) of water a day.

HOW TO CHOOSE A HEALTHY DIET

Foods	Choose more often	Choose less often
Meat, poultry, fish, shellfish, nuts and seeds	Lean cuts of meat trimmed of fat, poultry without skin, fish and shellfish, lean luncheon meat, tinned tuna, sardines, seeds, nuts.	Fatty cuts of meat, bacon and sausage, organ meats, fried chicken, high-fat luncheon meat
Eggs and dairy products	Live and natural yoghurt, low-fat yoghurt and semi-skimmed milk for adults, lower fat cheese (eg cottage cheese, Edam, low-fat Cheddar), boiled or poached eggs.	Cream, full-fat cheese (for adults), fried eggs, processed cheese.
Fats and oils	Soft polyunsaturated fats like margarine, sunflower, grapeseed, safflower, sesame, soya, rapeseed, corn, olive oils.	Saturated fats like butter, lard, suet, hard margarine.
Breads, cereals, pasta, rice, lentils, beans, biscuits, cakes	Wholegrain bread, wholegrain breakfast cereal, pasta and rice, dried beans and lentils, baked goods made with unsaturated oil or margarine, plain biscuits.	White bread, refined sugar-coated cereals, sugary biscuits, cakes, croissants.
Vegetables	Fresh or frozen, raw vegetables, salads, stir-fried vegetables, dark leafy greens and deep yellow or orange vegetables are particularly good.	Fried vegetables (eg chips, crisps), vegetables cooked with a lot of butter (eg mashed potato).
Fruits	Fresh, frozen, canned or dried fruit, pure fruit juice, eat a wide variety of fruits – citrus and berry fruits are particularly good.	Canned fruit in syrup, fruit juice with added sugar, fruit squash, creamy fruit deserts.
Sweet foods	Good quality ice cream, frozen yoghurt, fresh fruit lollies, cereal and dried fruit bars.	Sweets, creamy desserts, chocolates, jelly, sugary ice lollies, soft drinks.

CALCIUM

Calcium is important for the health and formation of bones and teeth and is therefore particularly important for growing children. Calcium is also important for smooth functioning of the muscles, including the heart. Many teenagers are significantly deficient in calcium, which is vital to help build healthy bones during the teenage period of rapid growth. Between 12 and 16 years for girls and 13 and 18 years for boys is a crucial period of bone and muscle growth.

Wheat bran, high-fibre cereals and the tannin in tea and coffee can hinder the absorption of calcium. So if you drink tea or coffee, leave a sufficient gap before or after your meal.

Dairy foods provide the best source of calcium. Two-thirds of a pint of milk a day or equivalent as yoghurt, cheese or milk puddings provides adequate calcium between the ages of one and five. Babies and young children should always be given full-fat milk and dairy products as they contain essential nutrients for early growth.

Other moderately good sources: *dark green leafy vegetables, tofu, sardines, sesame seeds and nuts.*

IRON

Iron deficiency is the commonest nutritional problem in the developed world. Iron's main function is to carry oxygen from the lungs to all the cells in the body. Iron also helps to increase our resistance to infection and aids the healing process. Lack of adequate iron can lead to anaemia, which will result in tiredness and lack of energy. Women, particularly teenage women, need to ensure there is enough iron in their diet as it is lost in the blood during menstruation. Girls who are dieting and those who switch to a vegetarian diet are particularly at risk.

There are two types of iron – one is found in foods of animal origin like red meat or oily fish and is easily absorbed by the body, and the other is found in foods of plant origin like green vegetables or wholegrain cereals and this is more difficult for the body to absorb. However, including a good source of vitamin C at the same meal, like a glass of fresh orange juice or sliced kiwi fruit and vegetables like sweet pepper or cauliflower, will help to increase the absorption of iron in non-meat sources. Also, if meat or fish is eaten at the same meal as the plant type of iron, the iron is better absorbed.

By mixing lean meat with dark green leafy vegetables you can improve the absorption of iron from the vegetables by about three times. Since the richest and best-absorbed sources of iron are meats and meat products, vegetarians should be careful to ensure they include enough iron-rich foods and vitamin C in their daily diet. Tea, coffee and bran reduce iron absorption.

Good sources: *red meat, particularly liver, oily fish (like salmon, sardines or mackerel), chicken or turkey (dark meat), pulses (like lentils, baked beans), fortified breakfast cereals, bread, green leafy vegetables, dried fruit (especially apricots).*

SMUGGLING EXTRA MILK

There are plenty of ways to add milk into other foods:
- make fruit milkshakes
- mash potatoes with plenty of milk
- make dishes with cheese sauce, eg cauliflower or cheese macaroni cheese
- sprinkle grated cheese on pasta
- offer yoghurt or fromage frais
- whip a half-set jelly with a tin of evaporated milk
- serve custard or good quality ice cream with puddings.

Vitamins

There are two types of vitamins: water-soluble – B complex and C; or fat-soluble – A, D, E and K. Water-soluble vitamins except for vitamin B12 cannot be stored in the body, so foods containing these should be eaten daily. They are destroyed by heat and dissolve in water, so foods containing these vitamins should not be overcooked. Fat-soluble vitamins are stored in the body, so excessive intake can be damaging.

Vitamin A:
(includes beta-carotene and retinol): important for growth, fighting infection, healthy skin and hair, strong bones, tooth enamel and night vision.
Good sources of beta-carotene: *carrots, tomatoes, red pepper, apricots, mangoes, cantaloupe melon, sweet potato and dark green leafy vegetables.*
Good sources of retinol: *liver, cheese, eggs.*

B complex vitamins:
important for growth, development of a healthy nervous system, food digestion. No foods except liver and yeast extract contain all of the vitamins in the B group.
Good sources: *meat, eggs, sardines, tofu, dark green leafy vegetables, nuts, yeast extract, dairy produce, wholegrain cereals, bananas.*

Vitamin C:
needed for growth and repair of body tissues, healthy skin and healing of wounds. It is also important because it helps the body to absorb iron.
Good sources: *citrus fruit, strawberries, blackcurrants, blackberries, kiwi fruit, sweet pepper, dark green leafy vegetables, potatoes.*

All in a day's food
Any of the following provides a day's vitamin C intake for the average adult.
1 medium-sized orange
1 medium sized mango
1 kiwi fruit
1 grapefruit
65 g (2½ oz) raw cauliflower
¼ red pepper, raw
1 medium glass freshly squeezed orange juice

Vitamin D:
this is nicknamed the sunshine vitamin because it can be manufactured by the body when the skin is exposed to sunlight. It is needed to absorb calcium and posphorus for healthy bones and teeth.
Good sources: *salmon, tuna, sardines, milk and dairy products, eggs, margarine.*

Vitamin E:
necessary for the maintenance of the body's cell structure and helps the body to create and maintain red blood cells.
Good sources: *vegetable oils, wheatgerm, nuts.*

VITAMIN C AND SMOKING
An average adult needs about 40 mg vitamin C per day. Smokers need up to three times as much because the chemicals from cigarettes destroy the vitamin.

HOME FREEZING OF COOKED FOODS

When you are preparing a recipe it takes only a little more effort to make enough for several meals. You can then serve part of the food freshly cooked and freeze the extra food in meal-size portions. Recipes in this book suitable for freezing are marked with an ❄.

■ Freeze food promptly as soon as it has cooled to room temperature.

■ Cool foods as quickly as possible before packaging – you can speed up the process by placing the container of food in a large pan of ice water.

■ Freeze and store foods at 0°F (-18°C) or less. It's a good idea to purchase a freezer thermometer that can withstand a wide range of temperatures and check the temperature of your freezer regularly.

■ Always re-heat food until piping hot and then allow to cool down before eating in order to kill off any bacteria.

■ Slightly undercook prepared foods. They will finish cooking when reheated.

■ Never re-freeze meals that have been frozen and never re-heat more than once.

■ Bread wrappers are not sufficiently moisture-vapour resistant to be used for freezing. Use proper freezer bags instead.

■ Label and date all packages.

SALT

Children should have no more than 4 g of salt a day but most eat twice as much. A high salt intake is linked to high blood pressure and heart disease, so try to limit the amount you add to food so that children don't develop a taste for it. Use herbs and spices to add flavour. About 75 per cent of the salt we eat comes from processed foods and is also hidden in foods like cereals, ketchup and bread.

HOW TO READ FOOD LABELS

When buying processed foods always look carefully at the labels for the list of contents.

■ Choose foods that are low in sugar, salt and saturated fat and do not contain monosodium glutamate, colouring or artificial flavours.

■ Ingredients are listed in order of decreasing weight, so if sugar or saturated fat appear near the top of the list, you may want to think again before buying that product.

■ Sugars can be listed in a variety of guises, among them dextrose, glucose, fructose and glucose syrup.

■ Sweetening food with honey, concentrated fruit juice or brown sugar is no better for your teeth than any other kind of sugar.

■ Often labels break carbohydrates into starch and sugars and it is useful to know that 4 grams of sugar makes 1 teaspoon.

■ Below is a chart to show acceptable content of fat, sugar, fibre and sodium per serving.

■ Most labels give the amount of sodium in grams per 100 g of food. To convert sodium to salt multiply the amount by 2.5, e.g. 1 g of sodium = 2.5 g salt.

Per 100 g/4 oz serving	A lot	A little
Fat	20 g or more	2 g or less
Saturates	5 g or more	1 g or less
Sugars	10 g or more	2 g or less
Fibre	3 g or more	0.5 g or less
Sodium	0.5 g or more	0.1 g or less

(approved by MAFF and the British Heart Foundation)

A Vegetarian Diet

More and more people are choosing to become vegetarian and a vegetarian diet can be very healthy. However, it is important not to give up meat without replacing it with other sources of the nutrients that meat contains, particularly iron, protein and B vitamins.

Animal proteins, including dairy products, contain all the amino acids that the body needs. However, soya is the only plant-based food that contains all the amino acids. In order to get a high-quality protein at each meal, you should try to include some dairy food or combine different non-animal proteins like grains and pulses, which do not contain all the essential amino acids. There are many vegetarian recipes included in this book.

A healthy vegetarian diet should contain staple foods like wholemeal bread, pasta, potatoes and rice, lots of fresh fruits and vegetables, nuts, seeds and pulses and low-fat non-animal sources of protein, eg tofu and low-fat dairy produce. Take care not to eat too much high fat dairy produce and eggs.

Some teenage girls who start dieting and also choose to become vegetarian, may cut out meat from their diet without replacing it with a suitable plant source of iron. This could cause problems as they are particularly prone to iron deficiency due to the loss of blood as they start their periods (see iron on page 14 for increasing the absorption of iron).

Vitamin B12 is vital for making DNA and is needed for the growth and division of cells. It is only found in foods of animal origin such as meat, poultry, fish, eggs and dairy products. Some breakfast cereals are also fortified with vitamin B12. Vegetarians can obtain sufficient vitamin B12 from eggs and dairy produce but vegans should take supplements or eat foods fortified with the vitamin.

NUTS

Small children can be allergic to a number of foods particularly peanuts, sesame seeds, milk, eggs, wheat, soya, fish and shellfish. Peanuts can trigger one of the worst allergic reactions – anaphylactic shock. The throat swells and breathing becomes difficult. In families with a history of any kind of food allergy, it is best to avoid all products containing peanuts until the child is 3 years old. If there is no allergic history, peanut butter can be used from six months. Because of the danger of inhalation, whole nuts should not be given to young children under 5 years of age.

Caramelised Onion and Gruyère Tart: see page 144 for recipe.

Breakfast

Suggestions

Breakfast

The first meal of the day is also the most important. It will probably have been at least 12 hours since your last evening meal and blood sugar levels will be low. If you attempt to skip breakfast then you may suffer various symptoms such as shakiness, headaches and lack of concentration. You will probably then feel hungry later in the morning and crave something sweet, which is your body telling you that it needs glucose fast. It is much better, particularly for children who have high energy and nutrient requirements and who have a long morning at school ahead of them, to start the day with a balanced nutritious breakfast. Here's how to make sure that your child gets a good balanced nutritious breakfast.

FRUIT AND FRUIT JUICE

Choose a wide variety of seasonal fruits. Make fresh fruit salads or a mixture of berries served with yoghurt and honey or prepare a colourful fruit plate. Berry and citrus fruits are particularly good in your child's diet. Breakfast should supply a good mix of starch and sugars. Sugar is best provided in the form of fruit or fruit juice, which is quickly broken down into glucose to raise energy levels as well as providing vitamin C, which helps to boost immunity.

BREAD, GRAINS, NUTS AND SEEDS

The type of carbohydrate you give your child affects their energy level and their ability to concentrate. Unrefined carbohydrates like porridge, muesli and wholegrain bread get broken down slowly into sugar in the blood, providing a steady supply of energy, whereas sugary refined cereals and white bread give a quick burst of energy followed by a drop in sugar levels, leaving your child tired, unable to concentrate and hungry. Adding extras like sunflower and sesame seeds, chopped nuts and dried fruit to cereals will boost their nutritional content.

The higher vitamin, mineral and fibre content of wholemeal bread makes it the healthiest choice; however, some children will only eat white bread. In the supermarket you can buy bread called Best of Both or Whole White, which looks like white bread but is made with one third wholemeal flour.

PROTEIN

Try to pick at least one calcium-rich protein food such as milk, yoghurt or cheese every day. Choose whole-milk rather than low-fat varieties for children under 5 unless they are overweight. Eggs are an excellent source of protein and iron for your child and are very versatile.

Eggs should be served to young children with the white and yolk cooked until solid.

BREAKFAST CEREALS

A bowl of cereal is a healthy start to the day for your child but you will need to choose carefully. Many of the cereals designed to appeal to children are highly refined and packed full of sugar (some contain almost 50% sugar). Ignore claims about added vitamins and minerals – vitamins are added to replace losses during processing. It is much better to choose whole-wheat cereals that are not coated in sugar like Weetabix, Ready Brek and porridge. Even if your child adds some sugar it will still be a lot less than the 4 to 5 teaspoons you might find in some cereals. Eating cereal also ensures your children get milk, which provides both protein and calcium.

> **TIP**
> Very fresh eggs will contain fewer bacteria than older eggs so try to find eggs that display the date on which they were laid. Elderly people, pregnant women and very young children should not eat lightly cooked or raw eggs.

Quick Breakfasts

FRUIT SALAD WITH HONEY YOGHURT DRESSING

Make a fruit salad using seasonal fruits and top with a mixture of Greek yoghurt and honey. Alternatively, make a fruit plate and serve with a bowl of yoghurt and honey for dipping.

STEWED FRUIT

Stewed fruit, like cooking apple cooked with a little brown sugar and cinnamon or rhubarb with some fresh orange juice and brown sugar, makes a nice change for breakfast. Alternatively, make a baked apple with honey, raisins and a knob of butter and serve it cold for breakfast.

BREAKFAST CEREAL PLUS

Adding fresh fruits or dried fruits like chopped dried apricots to breakfast cereals will give sweetness without the need for sugar.

FUNNY SHAPE FRENCH TOAST

Lightly beat together 1 egg and 30 ml (2 tbsp) of milk. Cut the bread into shapes using novelty cookie cutters and fry in butter until golden.

BOILED EGGS WITH SOLDIERS

Place the eggs in a saucepan, cover with cold water and place on a high heat. Bring to the boil and then reduce the heat to a simmer and cook for between 4 and 5 minutes. Serve surrounded by fingers of toast, spread with a little butter and Marmite. They are delicious dipped into the egg.

DRIED FRUIT COMPOTES

Many supermarkets stock a selection of ready-to-eat dried fruits. Put the fruit into a saucepan, cover with water, bring to the boil and simmer until soft (about 10 minutes). You can add a cinnamon stick to flavour the fruit if you like. It's also nice to mix in some fresh fruits like apples, pears or oranges. Add these towards the end of the cooking time as they will cook much faster. Fruit compotes can be made ahead and served cold.

TOAST WITH PEANUT BUTTER, HONEY AND BANANAS

Spread slices of toasted granary bread with peanut butter and a little honey and top with a thinly sliced banana.

FRUITY MILKSHAKES

Blend together fresh fruit and milk to make delicious milkshakes. Try combinations like fresh strawberries, banana and milk, peaches, nectarines or fresh dates and banana. For a richer milkshake, add a refreshing scoop of ice cream.

SCRAMBLED EGGS PLUS

Make scrambled eggs extra special by adding ingredients like chopped tomatoes, grated cheese or ham. These should be added one minute before the eggs are done.

BREAKFAST SUNDAE

Into a sundae glass spoon layers of yoghurt, fresh fruit (such as mixed berries) and crunchy breakfast cereal until the glass is full.

Strawberry and Banana Yoghurt Shake

Makes 1 tall glass

1 small banana, peeled and sliced
4 strawberries

30 ml (2 tbsp) orange juice
1 x 150 g (5 oz) pot vanilla yoghurt

Put the banana, strawberries and orange juice into a blender or food processor and purée. Add the yoghurt and purée until smooth.

Perfect Porridge

A bowl of porridge makes a satisfying and nourishing breakfast and will help to keep energy levels up until lunchtime. The soluble fibre in oats also helps to lower blood cholesterol levels. These extras will make porridge taste even better: ready-made apple, apricot or plum compote; maple or golden syrup; chopped banana and a little dark muscovado sugar; chopped dried fruit e.g. apricots; a chopped dessert apple, tossed in a pan with melted butter, brown sugar and cinnamon.

Makes 2 bowls
porridge

50 g (2 oz) porridge oats
460 ml (16 fl oz) milk (or water)

30 ml (2 tbsp) strawberry jam
blueberries or raspberries

Mix the oats with the milk or water in a saucepan. Bring to the boil and then simmer, stirring occasionally, for 5 minutes. Stir the strawberry jam in a bowl until it turns runny and then drizzle it in a spiral pattern on to the cereal. Add some blueberries to decorate the spiral pattern.

Muesli with Yoghurt, Honey and Fruit

Makes 1 portion

3 tablespoons muesli
1 x 150 g (5 oz) pot natural yoghurt
10 ml (2 tsp) honey

fresh fruit, such as raspberries,
peaches, blueberries

Simply mix together the muesli, yoghurt and honey and top with the fresh fruit. Larger fruits such as strawberries or peaches are best cut into small pieces.

Best-ever Banana Bread

This banana bread is wonderfully moist and is great for breakfast or lunchboxes. This keeps well but you can also wrap slices in plastic wrap and freeze in plastic freezer bags. Many children aren't keen on nuts, so you can omit them from this recipe. Nut allergies are also a very real problem (see page 17).

Makes 8 slices

100 g (4 oz) butter
100 g (4 oz) brown sugar
1 egg
450 g (1 lb) bananas, mashed
45 ml (3 tbsp) natural yoghurt
5 ml (1 tsp) vanilla essence

225 g (8 oz) plain flour
1 teaspoon bicarbonate of soda
1 teaspoon ground cinnamon
¼ teaspoon salt
100 g (4 oz) raisins
40 g (1½ oz) chopped pecans or walnuts (optional)

Pre-heat the oven to 180°C/350°F/Gas 4 and grease and line a 22 x 11 x 7 cm (8½ x 4¼ x 2¾ in) loaf tin. Beat the butter and sugar together until creamy then add the egg and continue to beat until smooth. Add the mashed bananas, yoghurt and vanilla essence.

Sift together the flour, bicarbonate of soda, cinnamon and salt and beat this gradually into the banana mixture. Finally, stir in the raisins and chopped nuts (if using). Bake for about 1 hour or until a cocktail stick inserted in the centre comes out clean.

TIP
If time is short in the morning, get some of the breakfast organised the night before. Have cereal ready in bowls, perhaps prepare a muesli and keep it in the fridge overnight and simply stir in some fresh fruit in the morning or bake some banana bread the day before and have it ready on the table. If your child is really rushed in the morning, let him take some portable food with him on the way to school like a banana, home-baked muffins or some dried apricots.

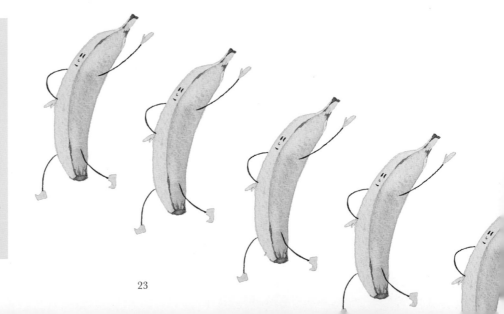

Cheesy Bread Shapes

These are good fun for children to make as they love to knead the dough and mould it into animal shapes. On a cool morning, you might like to consider warming them in the oven before eating.

Makes 6 bread shapes

225 g (8 oz) strong plain flour plus flour to dust
a pinch of salt
½ tablespoon fast action bread yeast
½ teaspoon caster sugar
1 teaspoon dried mustard powder
1 teaspoon vegetable oil
150 ml (¼ pint) water
50 g (2 oz) Red Leicestershire cheese, grated
25 g (1 oz) mature Cheddar cheese, grated
1 spring onion, finely chopped

To decorate

1 egg, beaten
currants
grated cheese
sesame seeds
poppy seeds

Sift the flour, mustard and salt into a bowl. Place the yeast in a mixing bowl, pour over the warm water, stir in the sugar and mix with a fork. Allow to stand until the yeast has dissolved and starts to foam (about 10 minutes). Stir in the oil and gradually mix in the flour mixture. If the dough is sticky, add a little extra flour. Transfer to a floured work surface and knead gently for about 5 minutes to make a smooth, pliable dough. Gradually knead the grated cheese and spring onion into the dough to give it a streaky effect.

Shape the dough into rolls or animal shapes and put them on to a greased baking tray. Cover loosely with a tea-towel and then put them in a warm place to rise for about 1 hour or until doubled in size.

Pre-heated the oven to 200°C/400°F/Gas 6. Brush the shapes with beaten egg and add currants for eyes. Sprinkle the tops with grated cheese, sesame seeds or poppy seeds. Bake in an oven for 15 to 20 minutes or until golden. They are done if they sound hollow when tapped underneath. Transfer to a wire rack to cool.

 The 'kids in the kitchen' symbol indicates where a recipe is suitable for children to make themselves.

Welsh Rarebit

This is the perfect mixture for a really tasty Welsh Rarebit. Traditionally Welsh Rarebit is flavoured with beer but you can use milk instead. To make fresh breadcrumbs simply tear a slice of white bread into pieces and whizz in a food processor.

Makes 2 portions

175 g (6 oz) mature Cheddar cheese, grated
2 tablespoons milk or beer
a few drops Worcestershire sauce
a generous pinch dried mustard powder

1 egg yolk, lightly beaten
3 tablespoons fresh white breadcrumbs
2 thick slices wholemeal or white bread
paprika, for sprinkling

Place the cheese and milk (or beer if using) in a saucepan over a low heat, stirring until melted. Add the Worcestershire sauce and mustard powder, and stir in. Remove from the heat and beat in the egg yolk. Stir in the breadcrumbs. Preheat the grill to hot. Toast the slices of bread and spread with the Rarebit topping, then sprinkle with paprika. Cook the Rarebits under the grill until golden and bubbling (about 2 minutes).

Cheese, Chive and Tomato Omelette

This is a delicious folded omelette, flavoured with chives and filled with fresh tomatoes and melted cheese. If you don't have any chives, then make a herb omelette using ¼ teaspoon mixed dried herbs. Eggs are a good source of protein and are rich in vitamins and minerals.

Makes 1 portion

2 eggs
½ tablespoon snipped chives
salt and freshly ground black pepper

15 g (½ oz) butter
2 tomatoes, skinned and roughly chopped
25 g (1 oz) Cheddar or Gruyère cheese, grated

Beat the eggs with the chives and season with a little salt and freshly ground black pepper. Melt the butter in a 20 cm (8 in) frying pan, add the beaten egg and chives and swirl the mixture around to coat the pan evenly.

When the edges of the egg begin to set, lift the egg with a spatula, tilt the pan towards the edge you have lifted and let the uncooked egg flow underneath the cooked portion.

Place the pan back on the burner. Spoon the tomatoes and grated cheese on to one side of the omelette. Fold over and cook for about 1 minute over a gentle heat until the omelette is set and the cheese is melted.

Perfect Pancakes

Pancakes for breakfast are a real treat and you can make delicious, really thin pancakes with this foolproof batter. Sprinkle them with lemon juice and dust with icing sugar or serve with maple or golden syrup and perhaps some fresh fruit. These pancakes can be made in advance, refrigerated and then re-heated just before serving. Pancakes also freeze very well. Interleave with non-stick baking paper, then wrap in foil and freeze for up to a month. Thaw at room temperature for several hours.

Makes 12 pancakes

100 g (4 oz) plain flour
a generous pinch of salt
2 eggs

300 ml (½ pint) milk
50 g (2 oz) melted butter

Sift the flour with a big pinch of salt into a mixing bowl, make a well in the centre and add the eggs. Use a balloon whisk to incorporate the eggs into the flour and gradually whisk in the milk. Stir the mixture until smooth but do not over mix.

Use a heavy bottomed 15-18 cm (6-7 in) frying pan and brush with the melted butter (either use a pastry brush or dip some crumpled kitchen towel into the butter to coat the base of the pan) and when hot, pour in about 30 ml (2 tbsp) of the batter. Quickly tilt the pan from side to side until you get a thin layer of batter covering the base of the frying pan. Cook the pancake for about 1 minute, then flip it over (you can use a spatula for this) and cook until the underside is lightly flecked with gold. Continue with the rest of the batter, brushing the pan with melted butter when necessary.

French Toast

Makes 2 portions

2 thick slices of day-old white bread
1 large egg

30 ml (2 tbsp) milk
25 g (1 oz) butter

Beat together the egg and milk and pour into a shallow dish. Cut the bread into triangles or cut out shapes using cookie cutters. Dip the bread into the mixture and fry in the butter until golden. Serve with fruit or a fruit compote (see Dried Fruit Compotes on page 21) and dust with a little icing or caster sugar.

Savoury Breakfast Muffins

Cheese and tomato on toast makes a nutritious breakfast and using split toasted muffins makes a nice variation. You can vary the toppings depending on what you have on hand in the kitchen. (*See photograph, opposite.*)

Makes 1 or 2 portions

1 muffin
a little butter or margarine
1 tomato, sliced thinly
salt and freshly ground black pepper
50 g (2 oz) Cheddar cheese, grated

Decoration (optional)
thinly sliced ham
2 cherry tomatoes
2 slices cucumber
1 black olive
slice of red pepper

Split and toast the muffin. Spread with a little butter or margarine. Arrange some thinly sliced tomato on top, lightly season and then cover with the grated cheese. Place under a pre-heated grill until lightly golden. If you wish, you can then have some fun decorating them to look like faces.

Apple and Carrot Breakfast Muffins

Here is a healthy and deliciously moist muffin that's bound to become a family favourite. These muffins are very easy to make and will keep well for up to 5 days. They are also great for lunchboxes or as a snack for any time of the day.

Makes 12 muffins

150 g (5 oz) plain wholemeal flour
50 g (2 oz) granulated sugar
25 g (1 oz) dried skimmed milk powder
1½ teaspoons baking powder
½ teaspoon cinnamon
¼ teaspoon salt
¼ teaspoon ginger
125 ml (4 fl oz) vegetable oil

60 ml (2 fl oz) honey
60 ml (2 fl oz) maple syrup
2 eggs, lightly beaten
2.5 ml (½ tsp) vanilla essence
1 large apple, peeled and grated
75 g (3 oz) carrots, peeled and grated
65 g (2½ oz) raisins

Pre-heat the oven to 180°C/350°F/Gas 4. Combine the flour, sugar, skimmed milk powder, baking powder, cinnamon, salt and ginger in a mixing bowl. In a separate bowl combine the oil, honey, maple syrup, eggs and vanilla essence. Beat lightly with a wire whisk until blended. Add the grated apple, carrots and raisins to the liquid mixture and stir well. Fold in the dry ingredients until just combined but don't over mix or the muffins will become heavy.

Line a muffin tray with paper cups and fill the muffin cups until two-thirds full. Bake for 20 to 25 minutes.

Fruity Homemade Muesli

So many of the breakfast cereals designed specifically for children are very high in sugar and low in nutrients. However, it's very easy to make your own delicious muesli using porridge oats, fresh and dried fruits and fresh fruit juices. There are now many delicious fresh fruit juices available in supermarkets, which can be used to soak and flavour the grains. This makes a nutritious alternative and you can add fresh fruit depending on the season. *(See photograph opposite)*

Makes 4 portions

150 g (5 oz) porridge oats
50 g (2 oz) toasted wheat germ
25 g (1 oz) each dried peaches and apricots, finely chopped
25 g (1 oz) raisins

375 ml (12 fl oz) apple and mango juice or apple juice
1 apple, peeled and grated
fresh fruit, such as strawberries, raspberries, peaches

Soak the muesli base or oats, toasted wheat germ and dried fruit in the juice for at least 20 minutes or overnight. Stir in the grated apple and the fruit of your choice.

Delicious Home-made Granola

This makes a wonderfully nutritious breakfast. It is delicious on its own or with milk or yoghurt and fresh fruit, and will keep for several weeks in an airtight container. *(See photograph, page 18.)*

Makes 10–12 portions

1 x 350 g (12 oz) jar honey
250 ml (8 fl oz) maple syrup
250 ml (8 fl oz) safflower or sunflower oil
2 teaspoons pure vanilla essence
400 g (14 oz) rolled oats (jumbo organic are best)
75 g (3 oz) sunflower seeds
75 g (3 oz) pumpkin seeds

40 g (1½ oz) bran
40 g (1½ oz) wheatgerm
75 g (3 oz) sesame seeds
100 g (4 oz) flaked almonds
40 g (1½ oz) desiccated coconut
175 g (6 oz) raisins
175 g (6 oz) currants or dried cranberries

Pre-heat the oven to 160°C/300°F/Gas 2. In a saucepan, warm together the honey, maple syrup, safflower or sunflower oil and vanilla essence. Combine the rolled oats, sunflower seeds and pumpkin seeds and stir into the warm honey mixture. Spread out on a large baking sheet and bake for 10 minutes, stirring halfway through. Remove from the oven, mix in the bran, wheatgerm and sesame seeds and bake for 15 minutes, stirring occasionally. Spread the flaked almonds and coconut on top, bake for another 15 minutes, stirring halfway through but still keeping the almonds on top. Finish off for about 4 minutes under a pre-heated grill, watching to make sure that it does not burn. Add the raisins and currants or cranberries. Allow to cool and transfer to an airtight container.

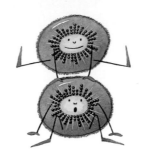

Soups, Snacks
and Lunchboxes

Soups, Snacks and Lunchboxes

PACKED LUNCHES

The nutritional quality of school meals varies hugely and if you are unhappy with your child's school meals and are unable to effect any real changes to be sure that your child is getting a good balanced meal, a packed lunch may well be the sensible answer. Often fussy eaters will find nothing that they like to eat in the school dining room and may end up eating very little for their lunch, with the consequence that they have no energy and lack concentration as the day wears on.

Warm conditions encourage the growth of bacteria so it's important to keep lunchboxes cool. For the summer months buy some ice packs that can be frozen overnight and then popped into an insulated lunchbox the next day to keep the food fresh. Alternatively, you could put a carton of juice in the freezer, transfer it to your child's lunchbox in the morning and by lunchtime it will have defrosted but will have helped to keep your child's food fresh.

TOP TIPS

● Use lots of different breads such as pitta bread, bagels, ciabatta, granary, etc. to make sandwiches. It's a good idea to have a small plastic container to put your sandwiches in so that they don't get squashed.

● Salads make a nice change from sandwiches: try Chicken Caesar Salad, Cherry Tomatoes and Mini Balls of Mozzarella or Turkey Salad with Pasta, Sweetcorn, Cherry Tomatoes and Spring Onion. Keep the salad dressing separate and let your child pour it over his salad himself so that it remains crisp.

● Avoid too many processed foods as they tend to contain few nutrients and too much salt, sugar, additives and saturated fat. If your child likes crisps but you don't want

him to fill himself up by eating a whole bag, put some in a small bag and tie the top. Try offering Twiglets, toasted seeds, honey-roasted cashew nuts or popcorn instead.

● Some foods like pasta salads and sandwich fillings can be prepared the night before to save time in the morning, or use leftovers from a pasta dinner or home-made soup.

● As the colder weather sets in it's a good idea to include something hot in a lunchbox. A wide-mouthed mini thermos flask would be ideal for serving up a delicious cup of home-made or good-quality bought soup like tomato soup which is both warming and nutritious. You could also put foods like baked beans in a flask.

● Give pure fruit juice, fruit smoothies or water. Some juice drinks contain less than 10% juice but have five teaspoons of sugar added, so check the label before buying. Also many low-sugar drinks contain artificial sweeteners.

● Many cereal bars contain more than 40% sugar and unlike the sugar in a bowl of cereal that gets washed away by the milk, this stuff sticks to your child's teeth.

● It is important to include fresh fruit in your child's lunchbox – you can cut up wedges of mango, melon, papaya and pineapple and pack them in a plastic container. Children tend to leave fruit that takes a lot of effort to eat so when giving something like clementines, peel them first and wrap them in cling film.

● Add a personal touch to your child's lunch, tuck in a note, stickers or joke or send a special treat labelled 'share with a friend'. Pack fun napkins, decorate lunch bags with stickers, or draw a face on a banana with a marker pen.

Lunchbox Suggestions

✓ Crunchy raw vegetables with a tasty dip like hummus or cream cheese and chive. Wrap sticks of carrot, cucumber, celery and sweet pepper in damp kitchen paper to keep them fresh. Cherry tomatoes are also popular. You can also thread a variety of vegetables onto small wooden skewers and intersperse with cubes of cheese and maybe some rolled-up thinly sliced ham or turkey. Wrap in foil or cling film.

✓ Miniature cheeses from the supermarket pick and mix selection.

✓ Yoghurt, probiotic mini-yoghurt drinks and fromage frais.

✓ A slice of pizza.

✓ Raisins and cashew nuts or honey-roasted cashew nuts.

✓ Dried fruit such as apricots. You can make fruit kebabs with different fruits, alternating fresh and dried.

✓ Include some home-baked cookies like the Best Ever Oatmeal Raisin Cookies on page 155. It's a good idea to get your child to help to bake with you.

✓ Hard-boiled eggs.

✓ Chicken skewers – there are quite a variety in this book (see Teriyaki or Easy Yakitori Chicken Skewers on pages 73 and 86) and they can be prepared the night before and refrigerated. These skewers are just as good cold as hot.

✓ Many supermarkets have individually wrapped snacks that are ideal to drop straight into your child's lunchbox. Try such items as small cartons of fruit purée, probiotic mini-yoghurt drinks, twin cartons of cream cheese with miniature breadsticks and miniature boxes of raisins.

✓ Vegetable crisps: you can buy packets of crispy carrot, parsnip, sweet potato and beetroot seasoned with sea salt.

✓ Oatcakes, rice cakes and other plain biscuits.

✓ Cereal bars.

✓ A piece of fruit.

✓ Home-made or bought soup in a flask.

Sandwich fillings

Try some of these suggestions:

✓ Peanut butter and strawberry or raspberry jam

✓ Peanut butter, honey and sliced bananas

✓ Strawberry jam and plain Quark cheese

✓ Cream cheese and cucumber

✓ Butter and Marmite, shredded lettuce, grated Cheddar cheese

✓ Peanut butter or chocolate spread and sliced banana

✓ Cheddar cheese with chutney, pickle or sliced pickled or fresh cucumber

✓ Prawns with mayonnaise mixed with a little tomato ketchup

✓ Hard-boiled egg mashed with a little soft margarine and mayonnaise and sprinkled with chopped salad cress, alfalfa sprouts or some finely chopped celery

✓ Hummus, grated carrot and sliced cucumber

✓ Cream cheese and chopped dried apricot

✓ Taramasalata

✓ Tuna mayonnaise with chopped celery

✓ Mashed sardines mixed with a little tomato ketchup

✓ Roast chicken or beef with salad in pockets of pitta bread

✓ Sliced turkey, salad and Swiss cheese

Lara's Lovely Onion Soup

My daughter Lara loves onion soup and this one has a delicious flavour as I allow the onions to caramelise to bring out their flavour. You can mix ordinary onions with red onions if you like. It's great comfort food on a cold winter's night.

Makes 8 portions

30 ml (2 tbsp) olive oil
50 g (2 oz) butter
550 g (1¼ lb) onions, thinly sliced
1 clove garlic, crushed
½ teaspoon granulated sugar
1.2 litres (2 pints) good beef stock

1 large potato, peeled and cubed
150 ml (¼ pint) dry white wine
salt and freshly ground black pepper
½ French loaf
75 g (3 oz) Gruyère cheese, grated

TIP

For winter, it's a good idea to include something hot in your child's lunchbox, so invest in a small Thermos flask that you could fill with soup. There are many delicious home-made soups to try, or perhaps heat up a small can of baked beans and use that to fill a Thermos flask.

Melt the oil and butter in a large casserole. Add the onions, garlic and sugar, and cook over a medium heat, stirring until the onions have browned. Reduce the heat to the lowest setting, cover the onions with a sheet of non-stick baking paper and leave the onions to cook slowly for 30 minutes.

Meanwhile, put 600 ml (1 pint) of the stock into a saucepan, add the chopped potato and cook for 10 to 12 minutes or until the potato is soft. Blend the potato with some of the stock in a food processor or blender. This will help to thicken the soup.

Remove the non-stick baking paper and pour the thickened stock, the remaining beef stock and the wine over the caramelised onions. Season, then stir with a wooden spoon, scraping the base of the pan to get the full flavour of the caramelised onions. Simmer gently uncovered for 30 minutes.

To make the cheesy French bread slices to float on top of the soup, first cut the loaf diagonally into 12 mm (½ in) slices and toast lightly on both sides. Pour the soup into individual oven-proof bowls and top each one with a slice of bread. Sprinkle the bread liberally with the grated cheese. Place the bowls under a hot grill until the cheese is melted and bubbling. Serve immediately.

Tasty and Healthy Vegetable Soup

A good home-made vegetable soup can be a great way to encourage reluctant vegetable eaters to eat more. This is one of my favourite combinations.

Makes 8 portions

25 g (1 oz) butter
1 medium onion, chopped
400 g (14 oz) carrots, peeled and chopped
225 g (8 oz) potato, peeled and chopped
1.2 litres (2 pints) good chicken or vegetable stock
150 g (5 oz) button mushrooms, chopped
1 celery stalk, chopped

1 clove garlic, crushed
½ teaspoon sugar
1½ teaspoons snipped fresh thyme or ½ teaspoon dried thyme
salt and freshly ground black pepper

Melt the butter in a large casserole or saucepan and sauté the onion until softened and lightly golden. Stir in the carrots and potato and cook, stirring, for 2 minutes. Pour over the stock and add the mushrooms, celery, garlic, sugar and thyme. Bring to the boil, then reduce the heat and cover and simmer for about 50 minutes. Liquidise in a blender and season to taste.

Nourishing Lentil Soup

Lentils are not generally very popular with children but here's a very tasty way to enjoy them. This nutritious soup has proved very popular with my young team of tasters, who never hesitate to give something the thumbs down if it doesn't appeal.

Makes 8 portions

25 g (1 oz) butter
1 medium onion, chopped
1 leek, white part only, finely sliced
1 clove garlic, crushed
225 g (8 oz) carrots, chopped
50 g (2 oz) celery, finely sliced

100 g (4 oz) red lentils
1 medium potato (about 150 g/5 oz), peeled and diced
2 tablespoons fresh chopped parsley
1.75 litres (3 pints) vegetable or chicken stock
salt and freshly ground black pepper

Melt the butter in a large saucepan and sauté the onion, leek, garlic, carrots and celery for about 10 minutes or until softened. Add the lentils, diced potato and parsley and pour the stock into the mixture. Stir and bring to the boil. Season with a little salt and freshly ground black pepper, cover and simmer gently for about 45 minutes. Purée in a blender to a thick, smooth consistency.

Thai-style Chicken Soup

Thai-style food tends to be very popular with children and this quick, easy-to-prepare soup is almost a meal in itself. Add more chilli if you want to spice it up a little.

Makes 4 portions

1 tablespoon light olive oil
150 g (5 oz) chopped onion
1 clove garlic, crushed (bash the garlic to make it easy to peel)
½ red chilli, finely chopped (approx. 1 tbsp)
1 chicken breast fillet, cut into thin strips

100 g (4 oz) broccoli
600 ml (1 pint) chicken stock
300 ml (½ pint) coconut milk
salt and pepper
150 g (5 oz) cooked rice (40 g/1½ oz uncooked weight)

Heat the oil in a pan and sauté the onion, garlic and chilli for 2 minutes. Add the strips of chicken and sauté for 2 more minutes. Cut the broccoli into small florets. Add the broccoli and chicken stock, bring to the boil and simmer for 4 minutes. Stir in the coconut milk and simmer for 2 minutes. Season to taste and stir in the cooked rice.

Mummy's Minestrone

Minestrone is a family favourite in our house. Sometimes, I leave out the baked beans and soup pasta and instead add a can of cartoon character pasta in tomato sauce, which seems to add to its child appeal.

Makes 8 portions

30 ml (2 tbsp) sunflower oil
1 medium onion, finely chopped
50 g (2 oz) leeks, diced
100 g (4 oz) carrots, diced
100 g (4 oz) potatoes, peeled and diced
100 g (4 oz) French beans, topped and tailed and cut into 12 mm (½ in) lengths

50 g (2 oz) diced celery
1.8 litres (3 pints) good chicken or vegetable stock
25 g (1 oz) tiny star-shaped pasta
100 g (4 oz) frozen peas or 100 g (4 oz) frozen baby broad beans
1 x 205 g (7 oz) can of baked beans

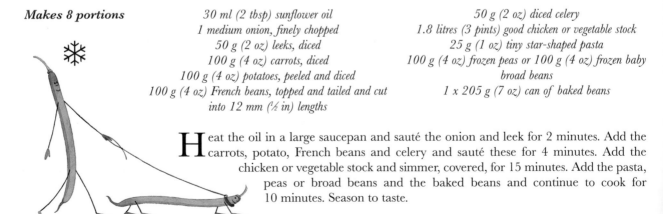

Heat the oil in a large saucepan and sauté the onion and leek for 2 minutes. Add the carrots, potato, French beans and celery and sauté these for 4 minutes. Add the chicken or vegetable stock and simmer, covered, for 15 minutes. Add the pasta, peas or broad beans and the baked beans and continue to cook for 10 minutes. Season to taste.

Mediterranean Tomato Soup

This tomato soup has a wonderful flavour and it's a great recipe to encourage children to eat more vegetables. Tomatoes are particularly rich in vitamin C and lycopene (the red pigment), which has been found to help protect against certain forms of cancer, in particular prostate cancer, so it's especially advisable for men to include tomatoes in their diet several times a week. Lycopene is released when tomatoes are cooked and better absorbed with a little oil.

Makes 6 portions

30 ml (2 tbsp) olive oil
25 g (1 oz) butter
2 medium onions, diced
2 medium carrots, peeled and diced
2 celery sticks, diced
1 clove garlic, crushed
1½ tablespoons roughly chopped basil

1½ tablespoons roughly chopped tarragon
1 bay leaf
500 g (1 lb 2 oz) ripe plum tomatoes, skinned,
quartered and de-seeded
1 x 400 g (14 oz) can of chopped tomatoes
15 ml (1 tbsp) tomato purée
600 ml (1 pint) chicken stock

Heat the olive oil and butter in a large saucepan and sauté the onion, carrots and celery for 2 to 3 minutes. Add the garlic, herbs and bay leaf and cook for 7 to 8 minutes. Add the fresh and canned tomatoes and cook over a low heat for about 15 minutes. Stir in the tomato purée and gradually add the stock. Cook over a medium heat for 15 minutes. Remove the bay leaf and blend in a food processor or blender. Season to taste.

Tuna Melt

Try this nutritious, tasty, quick and easy snack. If you wish you can use half-fat crème fraîche and Cheddar cheese. This is also good for breakfast.

Makes 2 portions

1 x 200 g (7 oz) tin tuna in brine
2 tablespoons tomato ketchup
2 tablespoons crème fraîche

1 or 2 finely sliced spring onions (optional)
2 English muffins
40 g (1½ oz) grated Cheddar cheese

Drain the brine from the tuna and flake into small pieces. Mix together with the tomato ketchup, crème fraîche and spring onions (if using).

Split the muffins and toast them. Spread with the tuna mixture and sprinkle with the grated Cheddar. Place the muffins under a pre-heated grill and grill until the cheese is golden and bubbling.

Cucumber Crocodile

This looks amazing, it's great for parties and it also makes a fabulous prop for your own children's healthy snacks. I like to use a variety of cheeses , but cubes of ham or chicken also work well on in place of the cheese. (*See photograph, opposite.*)

Serves 4–6

1¼ cucumbers
mixture of cheeses
1 carrot (optional)

fresh pineapple or 1 small can of pineapple chunks
cocktail sticks
2 cherry tomatoes

Cut a long strip from a carrot using a vegetable peeler. Cut this into a strip about 1½ cm/½ inch wide and cut along one side to form a serrated edge. These are the crocodile's teeth. Cut the quarter cucumber into two 3 cm-/1 inch-wide slices, cut these in half and then shape into feet with a triangular shape cut out of them. Attach these to the whole cucumber using cocktail sticks cut in half. Chop the cheese and pineapple into cubes. Thread cheese and pineapple cubes onto each cocktail stick and spear the sticks into the cucumber. Cut a cocktail stick in half and use the two halves to attach the cherry tomatoes to form the crocodile's eyes.

Bagel Fillers

Bagels are popular for a tasty snack or for your child's lunchbox. They are great with so many different fillings. If you like you can also toast the bagels.

Good bagel fillings
Cream cheese, smoked salmon, lemon juice
and black pepper
Pastrami and gherkins
Small prawns mixed with mayonnaise, a little tomato
ketchup, Worcestershire sauce and
sprinkled with paprika
Chopped cooked chicken with chopped hard-boiled
egg, sweetcorn, mayonnaise and
chopped sun-blush tomatoes

Crispy cooked rashers of streaky bacon
with a few crisp lettuce leaves, sliced tomato
and a little mayonnaise
Marmite and butter
Sliced turkey, Swiss cheese, tomato, salad
and salad dressing
Flaked tuna with sweetcorn, spring onion
and mayonnaise
Sliced ham and Gruyère cheese
Egg mayonnaise and salad cress

Turkey Pasta Salad

A quick and easy salad that is very nutritions. Great for lunchboxes or a light snack. This has a really nice dressing that children love! *(See photograph, page 32.)*

Makes 2–3 portions

50 g (1½ oz) pasta shapes
50 g (1½ oz) broccoli florets
100 g (3½ oz) turkey or chicken breast fillet, cooked and chopped
100 g (3½ oz) canned or frozen sweetcorn
2 tomatoes, skinned, de-seeded and chopped, or 6 cherry tomatoes, halved
2 spring onions, thinly siced

1 tablespoon toasted sesame seeds

Dressing
3 tablespoons light olive oil
1 tablespoon runny honey
1 tablespoon soy sauce
1 tablespoon freshly squeezed lemon juice

Cook the pasta in boiling, lightly salted water according to the instructions on the packet. Steam the broccoli florets for 5 minutes. Meanwhile, whisk together all the ingredients for the dressing.

Put the chopped turkey or chicken, sweetcorn, tomatoes and spring onions into a bowl together with the drained pasta and toss with the dressing.

Tortilla wraps make a nice change from ordinary sandwiches. Try fillings like:
- Cooked chicken, salsa and sour cream
- Hummus and grated carrot
- Sliced turkey with shredded lettuce, grated Cheddar cheese and salad cream

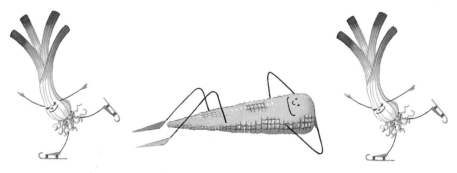

Mini Muffin Pizzas

These mini-pizzas are delicious. I have used a courgette and cherry tomato topping but you can choose any topping, perhaps adding some diced ham on top of the tomato sauce before covering with grated cheese. Otherwise, just make a simple cheese and tomato pizza without any extra toppings. You can double the quantity of tomato sauce and keep it in the fridge ready for when you want to make pizzas. You can also make these using chilled pizza dough bought in the supermarket, which you simply roll out and cut into circles. Follow the instructions on the packet.

**Makes 4
mini-pizzas**

*1 tablespoon olive oil
½ small onion, finely chopped (approx. 50 g/2 oz)
1 small garlic clove, crushed
100 ml (3½ fl oz) passata
½ tablespoon tomato purée
a pinch of sugar
a little salt and pepper
1 tablespoon fresh basil leaves,
torn into pieces (optional)*

2 English muffins, halved

Toppings
*sliced salami
pepperoni
diced ham and pineapple
sweetcorn
sweet pepper
mushrooms
sliced pitted olives
cherry tomatoes
basil*

*75 g (3 oz) grated Cheddar or mozzarella cheese,
or a mixture of both*

Heat the olive oil in a small saucepan and sauté the onion and garlic for 3 to 4 minutes. Add the passata, together with the tomato purée and seasoning and cook for approximately 2 minutes or until the mixture is thick enough to spread. Remove from the heat and stir in the torn basil leaves, if using.

Toast the split muffins and divide the tomato sauce between them. Choose your favourite topping and then cover with the grated cheese. Place under a pre-heated grill until golden and bubbling.

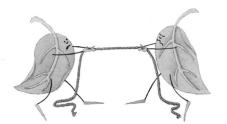

Buzzy Bees

This mixture is very tasty; if you like, you can simply roll it into balls and eat it plain. Also, instead of using flaked almonds for the wings, you could use white chocolate buttons. Older children will enjoy making these themselves because they are quick and easy to make and need no cooking.

Makes 10 bees

60 ml (4 tbsp) smooth peanut butter
15 ml (1 tbsp) honey
2 tablespoons dried skimmed milk powder
1 tablespoon sesame seeds
1 Weetabix, crushed

Decoration
1 tablespoon cocoa powder
rice paper cut into the shape of wings or flaked almonds
10 currants

Mix together the peanut butter and honey then blend in the remaining ingredients. Form heaped teaspoons of the mixture into oval shapes to look like bees. Dip a toothpick into the cocoa powder and press gently on to the bees' bodies to form stripes.

Press rice paper wings or flaked almonds into the sides of the bee. Cut the currants in half, roll between your finger and thumb to form tiny balls and arrange them on the bees to look like eyes. The bees can be stored in the fridge for several days.

Salad Bar with Soy Sauce Dressing

Salads and a jacket potato can easily become a main meal with the addition of ingredients like grated cheese, chopped egg or chopped chicken. Combined with some delicious freshly baked breads, which can now be bought in the supermarket, fresh fruit and ice cream, it makes an easy and popular meal for the whole family. Sometimes when I have a group of children over for lunch in the summer, I lay out a salad bar with bowls of different ingredients and a choice of dressings so that everyone can help themselves. The Dressing for Dinner sauce (opposite) is my favourite and is particularly popular with my children. Here are some ideas for your salad bar.

A variety of different lettuces
Cherry tomatoes
Cucumber
Grated carrots
Sweet peppers
Tiny florets of broccoli or cauliflower
Cooked French beans
Cooked sweetcorn
Hard-boiled egg
Toasted sunflower seeds
Avocado tossed in lemon juice
Pine nuts
Tuna fish
Grated cheese or chopped blue cheese
Cooked pasta
Chopped chicken or turkey

Soy Sauce Dressing
15 ml (1 tbsp) balsamic or wine vinegar
a good pinch of dried mustard
a pinch of caster sugar
15 ml (1 tbsp) soy sauce
freshly ground black pepper
60 ml (4 tbsp) light olive oil

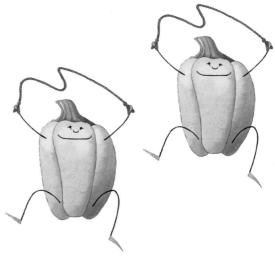

To make the dressing, mix together the first five ingredients, then whisk in the olive oil.

The Salad Bar with Soy Sauce Dressing is shown overleaf

Japanese Salad Dressing

This dressing is pure magic, and I can't make enough of it to please my children. It is based on the salad dressing served at a chain of popular American Japanese restaurants called Benihana. I use it to dress a mixed salad comprising crisp mixed lettuce, tomatoes, grated carrot, cucumber and sometimes thinly sliced radish. Once you've tried this recipe you will probably want to increase the quantities and keep a bottleful in your fridge.

Makes 6 portions

15 ml (1 tbsp) soy sauce
60 ml (4 tbsp) light crème fraîche
½ teaspoon minced or finely chopped ginger root

2 teaspoons caster sugar
30 ml (2 tbsp) rice wine vinegar

Combine the soy sauce, crème fraîche, ginger, caster sugar and vinegar with an electric hand-held blender and blend until smooth.

Dressing for Dinner

The secret of getting your child to enjoy eating salad is to make a seductive salad dressing. My children are all hooked on this Dressing for Dinner sauce and now prefer to come home to a plate of delicious salad vegetables than a bag of crisps and a chocolate biscuit.

Serves 5

25 g (1 oz) finely chopped onion
50 ml (2 fl oz) vegetable oil
30 ml (2 tbsp) rice wine vinegar
30 ml (2 tbsp) water
½ tablespoon chopped fresh ginger root
1 tablespoon chopped celery

15 ml (1 tbsp) soy sauce
7.5 ml (1½ tsp) tomato purée
7.5 ml (1½ tsp) sugar
5 ml (1 tsp) lemon juice
salt and freshly ground black pepper

Combine all the ingredients, except for the salt and pepper, in a blender or food processor and process until smooth. Season to taste.

TIP
Dressing for Dinner is also good mixed with a pasta salad comprising cooked pasta shapes, steamed cauliflower, French beans, sweetcorn, diced tomato and some diced, cooked chicken. It also makes an excellent salad for your child's lunchbox.

Bagel Snake

This is a fun way of arranging sandwiches and I find that bagels are popular with both children and their mums and dads. You can make the snake as long as you like depending on how many bagels you use and you can use a variety of toppings. I have chosen tuna and egg toppings, which are both nutritious, but, of course, there is an infinite variety of ingredients that you could choose, such as cream cheese and cucumber.

Serves 2

2 bagels

Tuna and cheese topping
1 x 200 g (7 oz) can of tuna in sunflower oil
(drained)
2 tablespoons tomato ketchup
2 tablespoons crème fraîche
2 spring onions, finely sliced

Egg mayonnaise with salad cress
2 to 3 hard-boiled eggs (10 minutes)
45 ml (3 tbsp) mayonnaise
1 tablespoon chives
3 tablespoons salad cress
salt and freshly ground black pepper

Decoration
a strip of red pepper
one stuffed olive, sliced
cherry tomatoes, halved
chives

S lice the bagels in half and then cut each half down the centre to form a semi-circle. Cut out the head of the snake from one of the pieces of bagel and the tail from another. Mix the ingredients for the tuna topping and mix the ingredients for the egg topping. Spread half the bagels with tuna and half with egg.

Decorate the tuna topping with halved cherry tomatoes and the egg topping with strips of chives arranged in a criss-cross pattern. Arrange the bagels to form the body of a snake. Then attach the head to the snake's body and arrange two slices of stuffed olive to form the eyes and cut out a forked tongue from the strip of red pepper.

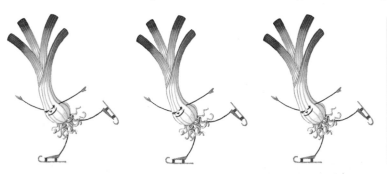

NOVELTY SHAPED SANDWICHES
Use cookie cutters to cut sandwiches into shapes like animals or gingerbread people. This really is a very simple way of transforming a simple sandwich into something special for your child. It can also be a particularly good way of tempting the reluctant sandwich eater, especially as the crusts tend to be removed.

Cheesy Pretzels

These make good snacks and children will have great fun twisting them into different shapes.

Makes 12 to 14 pretzels

250 g (9 oz) plain flour
25 g (1 oz) Cheddar cheese, grated
25 g (1 oz) butter, diced
2 teaspoons baking powder
1 teaspoon sugar
½ teaspoon salt
100 ml (3 fl oz) milk
1 egg, beaten

Toppings
coarse sea salt
sesame seeds
extra grated cheese

Pre-heat the oven to 200°C/400°F/Gas 6. Put the flour, cheese, butter, baking powder, sugar and salt in a mixing bowl and mix together with your fingers. Gradually add the milk to form a ball of dough. Sprinkle a clean surface with some flour and roll the dough around 3 or 4 times. Knead the dough by folding, pressing and turning and repeat this about 10 times.

Roll out the dough to a rectangle measuring about 25 x 18 cm (10 x 7 in). Cut the dough lengthways into strips each about 12 mm (½ in) wide. Pinch the edges and twist each strip into a pretzel shape. Put on a greased baking sheet, brush with beaten egg and sprinkle with coarse salt and sesame seeds or some extra grated cheese. Bake for 10 to 12 minutes or until golden.

A BALANCED LUNCHBOX

A packed lunch should contain:

✓ A high carbohydrate food, such as sandwiches or pasta salad
✓ Some protein, such as cheese, chicken drumstick or tuna
✓ Fresh fruit
✓ Something sweet and nutritious, such as a muffin, cereal bar or chocolate biscuit bar snack
✓ A drink, such as pure fruit juice, milk or milkshake.

Try to choose plenty of fresh foods, not too many highly refined foods.

Pasta

Annabel's 15-minute Tomato Sauce

There are now lots of wonderful ingredients available in most supermarkets like pesto and fresh basil, which can transform an ordinary tomato sauce into something very special. Vary the sauce by adding some sliced sautéed mushrooms.

Makes 4 portions

225 g (8 oz) spaghettini
30 ml (2 tbsp) olive oil
1 small onion, finely chopped
1 clove garlic, crushed
¼ to ½ teaspoon finely chopped red chilli
(optional)
2 x 400 g (14 oz) can of chopped tomatoes

30 ml (2 tbsp) red pesto
5 ml (1 tsp) balsamic vinegar
1 teaspoon caster sugar
salt and freshly ground black pepper
1 tablespoon fresh basil, torn into pieces
25 g (1 oz) Parmesan cheese, grated

Cook the spaghettini according to the instructions on the packet. Sauté the onion, garlic and chilli, if using, in the olive oil for about 5 minutes. Drain the juice from one of the cans of tomatoes and stir in the drained tomatoes and the second can of tomatoes and juice and all the other ingredients except the basil and Parmesan cheese and let simmer for 10 minutes. Stir in the basil and Parmesan cheese until melted.

Lara's Lasagne

This is one of my daughter Lara's favourite dishes and in winter it makes a good family meal and freezes well. Lasagne seems to be one of those dishes that is popular with most children. It provides a good source of iron and calcium.

Makes 6 portions

1 onion, chopped
1 clove garlic, crushed
½ red pepper, cored, de-seeded and chopped
15 ml (1 tbsp) olive oil
450 g (1 lb) lean minced beef
½ teaspoon mixed freeze-dried herbs
1 x 400 g (14 oz) can of chopped tomatoes,
drained
1 x 295 g (10 oz) can of condensed cream of
tomato soup
salt and freshly grated black pepper

Cheese sauce
50 g (2 oz) butter
40 g (1½ oz) flour
460 ml (16 fl oz) milk
a generous pinch of ground nutmeg
50 g (2 oz) Gruyère cheese, grated
25 g (1 oz) Parmesan cheese, grated

9 sheets fresh or no pre-cook lasagne

Pre-heat the oven to 190°C/375°F/Gas 5. Heat the oil in a large saucepan and sauté the onion, garlic and red pepper until softened. Add the beef and the herbs and sauté until the beef has changed colour. Add the remaining ingredients and cook over a medium heat for 15 to 20 minutes. Season to taste.

Meanwhile, to prepare the cheese sauce, melt the butter, stir in the flour and cook for 1 minute. Gradually whisk in the milk, bring to the boil and whisk until thickened and smooth. Season with the nutmeg and a little salt and pepper. Remove from the heat and stir in the grated Gruyère cheese until melted.

To assemble the lasagne, spoon a little of the meat sauce on to the base of an oven-proof dish 28 x 17 x 7 cm (11 x 6½ x 2¾ in). Cover with three sheets of lasagne. Divide the remaining meat sauce in half and cover the lasagne with half of the sauce. Spoon over a little of the cheese sauce.

Cover with three more sheets of lasagne and cover with the remaining meat sauce. Again spoon over a little of the cheese sauce but make sure that enough remains to completely cover the top layer of lasagne. Arrange the remaining sheets of lasagne on top and then spread over the remaining cheese sauce so that the lasagne is completely covered. Sprinkle over the Parmesan cheese and cook in the oven for 25 to 30 minutes.

Spaghetti with Plum Tomatoes and Basil

A really good home-made tomato sauce is always popular and it can be served with any type of pasta and some freshly grated Parmesan cheese. You can add a couple of tablespoons of chopped sunblush (semi-dried) tomatoes together with the fresh tomatoes if you want to bring out the flavour. The sauce can be frozen separately. *(See picture, page 54.)*

Makes 4 portions

❄

2 tablespoons olive oil	½ teaspoon balsamic vinegar
1 onion, peeled and chopped	½ teaspoon brown sugar
1 clove garlic, crushed	a handful of basil leaves, torn into pieces
4 ripe plum tomatoes, skinned, de-seeded and chopped	salt and freshly ground black pepper
	200 g (7 oz) spaghetti

Heat the oil in a saucepan and sauté the onion and garlic for 5 to 6 minutes until softened but not coloured. Add the remaining ingredients (except the spaghetti), cover with a lid and cook over a medium heat for about 20 minutes.

Meanwhile, bring a large pan of lightly salted water to the boil. Add the spaghetti and cook according to the timing instructions on the packet. Drain and serve topped with the sauce.

Orient Express

Stir-fries are easy and quick to prepare as everything is cooked in the same pan, and they make a great family meal. As a short cut you can buy a ready prepared selection of stir-fry vegetables from your local supermarket. This can also be made with 300 g (10 oz) of beef cut into strips instead of the chicken. If you have some large carrots, it's fun to cut the carrot slices into stars using mini cookie cutters. Serve with rice or noodles. For extra appeal, how about using some 'child friendly' chopsticks made from brightly coloured plastic which are joined at the top.

Makes 6 portions

2 chicken breasts cut into strips

Marinade
15 ml (1 tbsp) soy sauce
15 ml (1 tbsp) sake or sherry
5 ml (1 tsp) sesame oil
1 teaspoon cornflour

225 g (8 oz) pasta twirls
45 ml (3 tbsp) vegetable oil
2 eggs, lightly beaten
1 onion, finely sliced

1 clove garlic, chopped (optional)
100 g (4 oz) small broccoli florets
100 g (4 oz) baby corn, cut in half
50 g (2 oz) red pepper, cut into strips
100 g (4 oz) carrots, cut into stars or strips
75 g (3 oz) button mushrooms, sliced
2 tablespoons finely sliced spring onion
22.5-30 ml (1½-2 tbsp) oyster sauce
1 chicken stock cube dissolved in 6 tablespoons boiling water
freshly ground black pepper

Mix together the ingredients for the marinade and marinate the chicken for about 30 minutes. Cook the pasta in a large pan of lightly salted water according to the packet instructions.

In a frying pan, heat 7.5 ml (½ tbsp) of the oil and fry the eggs until set. Cut into strips and set aside. Then heat 15 ml (1 tbsp) of the oil in a wok or large frying pan and stir-fry half the onion and garlic for about 2 to 3 minutes. Add the chicken and marinade, and stir-fry until the chicken is cooked through. Remove the chicken and onion and set aside.

Heat the remaining oil in the wok or frying pan and stir-fry the rest of the garlic and onion for 2 to 3 minutes. Add the broccoli, baby corn, red pepper and carrots and stir-fry for about 5 minutes. Sprinkle over a little water while stir-frying the vegetables. Add the mushrooms and spring onions and cook for 2 to 3 minutes.

Return the chicken to the wok, add the oyster sauce and stock and continue to cook for 2 to 3 minutes, or until the vegetables are tender and the chicken cooked through.

Easy Bolognese Sauce

This is a very quick and easy way to make a bolognese sauce using a can of tomato soup as one of the ingredients. Since red meat provides the best source of iron, it's good to find some family favourites that include it and this pasta sauce is particularly appealing to children.

Makes 4 adult or 8 child portions

1 large onion, chopped
1 clove garlic, crushed
15 ml (1 tbsp) vegetable oil
500 g (1 lb 2 oz) lean minced beef
½ teaspoon mixed freeze-dried herbs

100 g (4 oz) button mushrooms, sliced
1 x 400 g (14 oz) can of chopped tomatoes
1 x 295g (10 oz) can of condensed cream of tomato soup
400 g (14 oz) spaghetti

Sauté the onion and garlic in the oil for 2 to 3 minutes. Add the beef and the herbs and sauté until the beef has changed colour. Add the sliced mushrooms and sauté for 2 minutes. Add the remaining ingredients and cook over a medium heat for about 15 minutes. Season to taste. Meanwhile, cook the spaghetti in a large pan of lightly salted water according to the instructions on the packet. Mix the cooked pasta with the bolognese sauce and serve.

Three-cheese Macaroni

Pasta provides a good source of complex carbohydrate so this macaroni will boost your child's energy level as well as providing a good source of protein and calcium. If you like, you could mix in some sliced shredded ham or chopped bacon.

Makes 3 portions

150g (5½ oz) macaroni
30 g (1 oz) butter
30 g (1 oz) plain flour
300 ml (10½ fl oz) milk

40 g (1½ oz) Parmesan cheese, grated
60 g (2 oz) Gruyère cheese, grated
6 tbsp mascarpone cheese
salt

Cook the macaroni according to the instructions on the packet in plenty of boiling salted water. Melt the butter in a pan, stir in the flour and cook for 1 minute. Gradually add the milk, stirring over a low heat for 5–6 minutes. Take off the heat, stir in the Parmesan and Gruyère until melted then stir in the mascarpone.

Drain the pasta and return to the pan. Pour over the cheese sauce and heat through gently.

Lasagne with Spinach, Cheese and Tomato

This is my favourite vegetarian lasagne. If you can find sheets of fresh lasagne, I think they taste better than dried, and some supermarkets stock them in the chilled cabinet. If using the dried lasagne, you may need to cook this for 5 minutes longer and make sure that the lasagne is completely covered with sauce or it will dry out.

Makes 4 portions

Tomato sauce
1 onion, chopped
1 clove garlic, crushed
15 ml (1 tbsp) olive oil
30 ml (2 tbsp) tomato purée
2 x 400 g (14 oz) cans of chopped tomatoes
1 tablespoon fresh chopped parsley
1 tablespoon torn basil leaves
1 teaspoon dried oregano
½ teaspoon sugar
salt and freshly ground black pepper

225g (8 oz) frozen or 450g (1 lb) fresh
spinach
15 g (½ oz) butter
175 g (6 oz) cottage cheese
1 egg, lightly beaten
30 ml (2 tbsp) double cream
25 g (1 oz) Parmesan cheese, grated
15 g (½ oz) Gruyère cheese, grated
6 sheets fresh lasagne or dried no pre-cook
lasagne
125 g (4½ oz) Mozzarella cheese, grated

Pre-heat the oven to 180°C/350°F/Gas 4. To make the tomato sauce, sauté the onion and garlic in the olive oil until softened. Add the tomato purée and sauté for 1 minute. Drain and discard the juice from the cans of tomatoes and add the tomatoes to the sautéed onions. Add all the remaining ingredients and simmer uncovered for 10 minutes. Season to taste.

Meanwhile, to prepare the spinach and cheese layer, cook the spinach, drain thoroughly and then sauté in the butter for a couple of minutes. In a food processor, blend together the spinach, cottage cheese, egg, double cream and Parmesan cheese. Season with a little black pepper.

To assemble the lasagne, spread a thin layer of the tomato sauce over the base of a fairly deep oven-proof dish measuring about 23 x 15 cm (9 x 6 in). Lay two sheets of lasagne on top. Cover with half the spinach mixture, a third of the Mozzarella cheese and a third of the tomato sauce. Again, lay two sheets of lasagne on top, spoon the remaining spinach mixture on top and then cover with a third of the Mozzarella cheese and a third of the tomato sauce.

Lay the remaining two sheets of lasagne on top, cover with the remaining tomato sauce and Mozzarella cheese and then sprinkle the extra Gruyère cheese over the top. Bake in the oven for about 25 minutes.

Spaghettini with Spring Vegetables

Since pasta is generally so popular with children it's a good idea to combine it with foods that they are not so keen on eating. Here I have chosen some brightly coloured diced vegetables to make a delicious sauce for linguine or spaghetti.

Makes 4 portions

250 g (9 oz) spaghettini (thin spaghetti)
2 tablespoons vegetable oil
1 onion, finely chopped
1 clove garlic, crushed
½–1 teaspoon grated fresh ginger
150 g (5½ oz) carrots, finely diced
100 g (4 oz) finely diced red pepper
150 g (5½ oz) courgettes, finely diced
3 fresh tomatoes, peeled, de-seeded and chopped

4 spring onions, finely sliced
350 ml (12 fl oz) chicken stock
2 tablespoons soy sauce
1 tablespoon oyster sauce
1 tablespoon sweet chilli sacue
salt and freshly ground black pepper

freshly shaved Parmesan cheese (optional)

Cook the spaghettini in a large saucepan of lightly salted boiling water according to the instructions on the packet. Drain and set aside. Heat the oil in a wok or frying pan and sauté the onion and garlic for 3 minutes, stirring occasionally. Add the carrots, red pepper and courgette and cook, stirring occasionally, for 4 minutes. Add the tomatoes and spring onion and cook, stirring, for 2 minutes. Pour in the chicken stock, soy sauce, oyster sauce and sweet chilli sauce and cook for 1 minute. Season to taste. Drain the pasta and toss with the sauce. Serve with some freshly shaved Parmesan cheese.

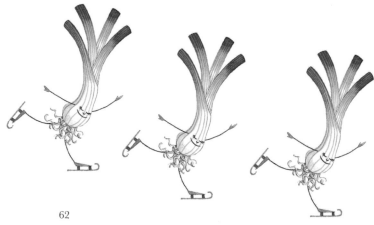

Bow-tie Pasta with Peas and Prosciutto

Here is a simple and quick pasta dish that tends to be popular with young children. You could also add a little crème fraiche or double cream to the sauce if you like. The garlic is optional in this dish because it is especially pronounced; if you or your children aren't too keen on garlic, feel free to omit it.

Makes 2 portions

15 ml (1 tbsp) olive oil
25 g (1 oz) butter
1 onion, finely chopped
1 clove garlic, crushed
75 g (3 oz) frozen peas

1 tablespoon chopped fresh parsley
125 ml (4 fl oz) chicken stock40 g (1½ oz)
prosciutto, finely diced
200 g (7 oz) bow-tie pasta
2 tablespoons freshly grated Parmesan cheese

Heat the olive oil and a small knob of the butter and sauté the onion and garlic (if using) for about 8 minutes or until softened. Add the peas, cook for 1 minute, then stir in the parsley and chicken stock. Bring to the boil, then reduce the heat and cook for 4 to 5 minutes. Stir in the prosciutto.

Meanwhile, cook the pasta in a large pan of lightly salted water according to the instructions on the packet. Drain the pasta, return to the warm pan, add the remaining butter and toss until it melts. Stir in the grated Parmesan cheese. Re-heat the peas and prosciutto and toss with the cooked pasta. Serve with some extra freshly grated Parmesan cheese if you wish.

Penne with Chicken, Tomatoes and Basil

There is a lovely mixture of flavours in this tasty chicken and pasta dish and it's very quick and easy to put together.

Makes 4 portions

200 g (7 oz) penne pasta
15 ml (1 tbsp) olive oil
a knob of butter
2 shallots or 1 small onion, finely chopped
25 g (1 oz) pine kernels
2 boneless chicken breasts, thinly sliced into strips

50 g (2 oz) sunblush tomatoes, drained and sliced
150 ml (¼ pint) chicken stock
150 ml (¼ pint) crème fraîche
25 g (1 oz) Parmesan cheese, grated
salt and freshly ground black pepper
2 tablespoons shredded basil leaves

Cook the pasta in a large pan of lightly salted water according to the instructions on the packet, drain and set aside. Meanwhile, heat the oil and butter in a large frying pan and sauté the shallots or onion and pine kernels for about 5 minutes, stirring occasionally. Add the strips of chicken and sauté, stirring occasionally, for about 5 minutes. Add the sunblush tomatoes and cook for 1 minute.

Pour the chicken stock into the frying pan and bring to the boil. Stir in the crème fraîche and Parmesan cheese and season with a little salt and freshly ground black pepper. Drain the pasta, toss with the sauce and stir in the fresh basil.

PRESERVING VITAMIN CONTENT

Many commercially frozen vegetables and fruits, such as peas, spinach, sweetcorn and berry fruits are frozen within 2 to 3 hours of being picked, thus ensuring that they retain their vital nutrients. In fact, fresh vegetables and fruits that have been stored for several days can sometimes contain fewer nutrients than the frozen variety.

The best method of cooking to retain maximum nutrients is steaming, microwaving or stir-frying. Boiled broccoli retains only 35% of its vitamin C as opposed to 72% when it is steamed or microwaved. If you want to boil vegetables, cook them in a small amount of water (just enough to cover the vegetables) and do not overcook. Scrub or wash fruit and vegetables rather than peeling them, as most of the nutrients lie just beneath the surface. When possible, try to buy organic fruit and vegetables. Vitamin C dissolves in water so avoid standing fruit and vegetables in water.

Vegetable Tagliatelle

This is a lovely light sauce with vegetables, cherry tomatoes and shredded gem lettuce, which can be served with almost any kind of pasta. It is a particularly good summer pasta recipe.

Makes 4 portions

200 g (7 oz) tagliatelle
15 ml (1 tbsp) olive oil
1 onion, finely chopped
1 clove garlic, finely chopped
1 small yellow pepper, cut into strips
100 g (4 oz) broccoli florets
1 medium courgette, sliced diagonally and cut

into semi-circles
125 ml (4 fl oz) light crème fraîche
125 ml (4 fl oz) vegetable stock
8 cherry tomatoes, halved
75g (3 oz) Parmesan cheese, grated
salt and freshly ground black pepper

Cook the tagliatelle in a large pan of lightly salted boiling water according to the directions on the packet. Heat the olive oil in a heavy-bottomed saucepan and sauté the onion and garlic for 1 minute. Add the yellow pepper, broccoli and courgette and sauté for about 8 minutes or until tender. Stir in the crème fraîche and the vegetable stock and bring to a simmer. Stir in the cherry tomatoes and simmer for 1 minute, then stir in the Parmesan cheese and season to taste. Toss the drained tagliatelle with the sauce. Serve with extra Parmesan cheese to sprinkle on top if you wish.

Turkey Bolognese

A tasty, quick and easy sauce for pasta. You could also make this using minced chicken.

Makes 4 portions

1 large onion, finely chopped
1 clove garlic, finely chopped
1 small red pepper, finely diced
30 ml (2 tbsp) vegetable oil
500 g (1 lb 2 oz) minced turkey
1 medium carrot, peeled and grated
1 x 400 g (14 oz) can of chopped tomatoes

1 chicken stock cube dissolved in 150 ml
(¼ pint) boiling water
15 ml (1 tbsp) Tomato Ketchup
1 tbsp fresh sage or ½ tsp dried sage
½ tbsp fresh thyme leaves or ¼ tsp dried thyme
salt and freshly ground black pepper
350 g (12 oz) spaghetti or penne

Sauté the onion, garlic and red pepper in the vegetable oil for 3 to 4 minutes. Add the turkey mince and stir until it changes colour, breaking up any lumps with a fork. Add the remaining ingredients, bring to the boil and then simmer uncovered, stirring occasionally, for 30 minutes. Meanwhile, cook the pasta according to the instructions on the packet, drain and toss with the sauce.

Tagliatelle with Prawns and Vegetables

I often make this for my own supper as two of my favourite foods are pasta and prawns. It also makes an excellent vegetable pasta dish without the prawns.

Makes 4 portions

200 g (7 oz) tagliatelle
a knob of butter
425 ml (¾ pint) chicken stock
5 ml (1 tsp) lemon juice
175 g (6 oz) cauliflower, cut into small florets
1 medium carrot, cut into matchsticks
50 g (2 oz) French beans or mangetout, trimmed
25 g (1 oz) butter
1 small onion, finely chopped

1 small garlic clove, crushed
100 g (4 oz) small courgettes, cut into matchsticks
175 g (6 oz) cooked and peeled king prawns either fresh or frozen and defrosted
1 tablespoon chopped fresh parsley
salt and freshly ground black pepper
1 tablespoon cornflour
60 ml (4 tbsp) light crème fraîche
25 g (1 oz) Parmesan cheese, grated

Cook the tagliatelle in a large saucepan of lightly salted water according to the instructions on the packet. When it is just tender, drain, add the knob of butter and toss the warm pasta with the butter. Set aside.

Put the chicken stock and lemon juice into a saucepan, bring to the boil, add the cauliflower, carrots and French beans or mangetout and cook over a medium heat for about 6 minutes or until the vegetables are just tender. Strain the vegetables, reserving the stock for later use.

Melt the butter in a frying pan, add the onion and garlic and sauté for 3 to 4 minutes. Add the courgettes and continue to cook for 3 to 4 minutes. Cut the prawns in half and add together with the parsley and the drained vegetables, lightly season and cook for 2 to 3 minutes or until heated through.

Mix a little of the reserved stock with the cornflour and heat the remaining stock in a saucepan. Mix the cornflour liquid into the remaining stock and cook, stirring for about 3 minutes or until the sauce thickens. Remove from the heat and stir in the crème fraîche. Toss the tagliatelle with the vegetables and sauce until well mixed. Serve with grated Parmesan cheese.

Scarlett's Pasta

This pasta dish is a great favourite with my children, especially Scarlett, who loves both pasta and salami. You could also use sliced sausage instead of salami if you prefer.

Makes 4 portions

2 shallots, finely chopped
½ small red pepper, chopped
15 ml (1 tbsp) olive oil
1 x 400 g (14 oz) can of chopped tomatoes, drained
180 ml (6 fl oz) strong chicken stock

225 g (8 oz) pasta
1 tablespoon fresh basil, shredded
1 tablespoon Parmesan cheese, grated
100 g (4 oz) salami, cut into strips
salt and freshly ground black pepper

Sauté the shallots and red pepper in the olive oil for about 5 minutes or until softened. Stir in the tomatoes and sauté for 2 minutes, then add the stock and simmer for about 10 minutes. Meanwhile, cook the pasta according to the instructions on the packet. When cooked, stir in the basil, Parmesan cheese and salami, heat through and season to taste. Drain the pasta and toss with the sauce.

VERY QUICK AND EASY PASTA SAUCE

For a simple sauce that tastes delicious, simmer 300 ml (½ pint) single cream with 50 g (2 oz) butter and seasoning. Toss with freshly cooked pasta like tagliatelle and fresh Parmesan cheese.

Poultry

Chicken Balls in Sweet and Sour Sauce

The grated apple adds a delicious flavour to these chicken balls which makes them appealing to children. They also make good finger food on their own. Alternatively, use minced meat to make meatballs in sweet and sour sauce.

Makes 4 portions

2 large chicken breasts, cut into chunks
1 onion, finely chopped
1 tbsp parsley
50 g (2 oz) fresh white breadcrumbs
1 large Granny Smith apple, peeled and grated
10 ml (2 tsp) chicken stock, dissolved in 5 ml (1 tsp) boiling water
flour for coating
vegetable oil for frying

Sweet and sour sauce
1 onion, finely chopped
1 small red pepper, de-seeded and chopped
22.5 ml (1½ tbsp) vegetable oil
1 x 400 g (14 oz) can of chopped tomatoes
15 ml (1 tbsp) tomato purée
150 ml (5 fl oz) pineapple juice
5 ml (1 tsp) brown sugar
5 ml (1 tsp) malt vinegar
5 ml (1 tsp) soy sauce

Using your hands, squeeze out some of the excess liquid from the grated apple. Mix together the chicken, onion, parsley, breadcrumbs, grated apple and chicken stock and chop in a food processor for a few seconds. Season with a little salt and pepper. With your hands, form into about 20 balls, roll in flour and fry in shallow oil until lightly golden (about 10 minutes). For the sauce, sauté the onion and sweet pepper in the oil until softened. Add the rest of the ingredients, plus freshly ground black pepper, bring to the boil and simmer, covered, for 15 minutes. Pour over the balls and serve with rice.

Tasty Satay Chicken Skewers

Makes 8 skewers

2 chicken breasts, each cut lengthways into 4 strips

2 tablespoons coconut milk
chopped coriander, to garnish

Marinade
1 tablespoon soy sauce
1½ tablespoons lime juice
1 tablespoon peanut butter
1 tablespoon runny honey
½ teaspoon mild curry powder
1 clove garlic, crushed

Combine the marinade ingredients. Place the chicken strips in the marinade and leave for at least 30 minutes. Remove the chicken and reserve the marinade. Thread the chicken strips onto pre-soaked bamboo skewers. Brush a griddle plan with a little oil and heat until hot. Sear the outside of the chicken, then reduce the heat and cook for 3 to 4 minutes on each side or until cooked through. To make the sauce, put the reserved marinade into a small saucepan. Bring to the boil, add the coconut milk and cook for 1 minute. Scatter chopped coriander over the skewers and serve with the sauce.

Annabel's Tasty Chicken Skewers

These skewers can also be interspersed with some vegetables, such as chunks of red pepper, onion or some button mushrooms. Brush the vegetables with the marinade before cooking the skewers. Alternatively, make skewers with chicken only and serve with boiled rice and stir-fry chopped onion and diced red and yellow peppers in some olive oil and stir into the cooked rice to give it both colour and flavour.

Makes 4 portions

4 chicken breasts cut into chunks
60 ml (4 tbsp) soy sauce
40 g (1½ oz) light muscovado sugar

15 ml (1 tbsp) lime or lemon juice
15 ml (1 tbsp) vegetable oil
1 clove garlic, crushed

Put the soy sauce and sugar into a small saucepan and gently heat, stirring until the sugar has dissolved. Remove from the heat, stir in the lime juice, vegetable oil and garlic. Marinate the chicken for at least 1 hour or overnight. Soak 8 bamboo skewers in water to prevent them from getting scorched. Thread the chunks of chicken on to the skewers and cook under a pre-heated grill for 4 to 5 minutes each side, basting occasionally with the marinade until cooked through.

Teriyaki Chicken Skewers

Marinated chicken skewers make an easy to prepare and very tasty meal. They are also good cooked on a barbecue.

Makes 4 portions

4 chicken breasts

Marinade
2 tablespoons soy sauce
1 teaspoon sesame oil

1 tablespoon rice wine vinegar
3 teaspoons runny honey
1 clove garlic, crushed
1 cm (½ inch) piece root ginger, peeled and grated (optional)

Combine the ingredients for the marinade. Cut each chicken breast into 4 strips and marinate for at least 30 minutes. Soak eight bamboo skewers in water to prevent them scorching. Thread the chicken strips onto the skewers in the shape of a wiggly snake, then cook under a pre-heated grill for 4 to 5 minutes each side.

The Teriyaki Chicken Skewers are shown overleaf

Chicken Piccata

Here are tender breasts of chicken cooked in a delicious, quick and easy to prepare Chinese-style sauce.

Makes 2 portions

2 boneless chicken breasts

Marinade
15 ml (1 tbsp) lemon juice
15 ml (1 tbsp) water
1 tablespoon finely chopped onion

plain flour
salt and freshly ground black pepper
30 ml (2 tbsp) vegetable oil

Sauce
250 ml (8 fl oz) chicken stock
10 ml (2 tsp) soy sauce
5 ml (1 tsp) sesame oil
1 tablespoon sugar
1 teaspoon cider vinegar
1 tablespoon cornflour
ground white pepper
1 spring onion, thinly sliced

Rinse the chicken and pat dry with paper towels. Place the chicken breasts under a layer of plastic wrap. Using the flat side of a meat mallet, pound until quite thin and cut each breast in half. Remove the plastic wrap and place the chicken in a shallow dish. Mix together the lemon juice and water, add the chopped onion and marinate the chicken in this for 30 minutes. Remove the chicken pieces and discard the marinade. Dip the chicken in seasoned flour. Heat the vegetable oil in a frying pan or wok and sauté the chicken for about 5 minutes on each side or until lightly browned and cooked through. Meanwhile, put all the ingredients for the sauce into a saucepan and bring to the boil. Cook over a medium heat, stirring until thickened. Drain away any excess oil from the pan in which the chicken was cooked, pour the sauce over the cooked chicken and heat through.

Chicken Fajitas

These are fun for children to eat with their hands, wrapped in a colourful napkin. They are also good cold in a lunchbox.

Makes 3 large or
4 small tortillas

1 tablespoon olive oil
1 small clove garlic, crushed
50 g (2 oz) red onion, sliced
25 g (1 oz) red pepper, cored, de-seeded and
cut into strips
1 chicken breast (approx. 150 g/5½ oz),
cut into strips
½ red chilli, finely chopped

½ teaspoon balsamic vinegar
1 x 200 g (7 oz) can chopped tomatoes
1 tablespoon chopped fresh oregano, or
1 teaspoon dried oregano
salt and freshly ground black pepper
3 large or 4 small tortillas
a little shredded lettuce
3 tablespoons soured cream

Heat the oil in a wok or frying pan, add the garlic, onion and red pepper and stir-fry for 3 minutes. Add the chicken and chilli and stir-fry for another 3 minutes. Add the balsamic vinegar and cook for a few seconds, then add the chopped tomatoes, oregano and seasoning. Cook for about 4 minutes or until the mixture has thickened.

To assemble, heat the tortillas in the microwave or frying pan according to the packet instructions. Place some of the chicken mixture along the centre of each tortilla, add some shredded lettuce and a little soured cream and roll up. Serve immediately.

Chicken Karmel

This sweet and sour chicken recipe is a great favourite with children and my family loves it. Serve with fluffy white rice. To make eating fun you can buy child-friendly plastic chopsticks that are joined at the top so that they only need to be squeezed together to pick up food. This recipe would be perfect for these as everything is cut into bite-sized pieces. If your child isn't keen on green beans or baby sweetcorn, use different vegetables or simply leave them out. *(See page 70.)*

Makes 4 portions

2 tablespoons vegetable oil
250 g (9 oz) chicken breasts, cut into bite-sized cubes

2 tablespoons vegetable oil
75 g (3 oz) carrot, cut into matchsticks
50 g (2 oz) baby corn, sliced in half lengthways then in half across
50 g (2 oz) fine green beans, topped and tailed and cut in half
2 spring onions, finely sliced
salt and freshly ground black pepper

Batter
1 egg yolk
1½ tablespoon cornflour
1 tablespoon milk

Sweet and sour sauce
1 tablespoon soy sauce
2 tablespoons tomato ketchup
2 tablespoons rice wine vinegar
2 tablespoons caster sugar
½ teaspoon sesame oil

In a small bowl, beat together the egg yolk, cornflour and milk to make a thin batter. Heat 2 tablespoons of oil in a wok, dip the chicken into the batter, then fry for 3 to 4 minutes until golden. Remove from the wok and set aside.

Meanwhile, mix together all the ingredients for the sweet and sour sauce. Heat two tablespoons of vegetable oil in a wok and stir-fry the carrot, baby corn and green beans for 2 minutes. Add the sauce, bring to the boil and cook for 2 minutes. Remove from the heat and stir in the spring onions. Add the chicken to the vegetables and heat through. Season to taste.

Turkey Burgers

These turkey burgers can also be eaten sandwiched between a bun and layered with salad and tomato sauce. Sometimes, children prefer these without herbs so you can leave them out of their portions. (*See photograph opposite*)

Makes 12 burgers

450 g (1 lb) turkey breast, roughly chopped, or minced turkey
1 onion, finely chopped
1 tablespoon fresh chopped thyme or oregano or ½ teaspoon dried
1 tablespoon fresh chopped parsley
1 apple, peeled and grated (squeeze out excess juice)

50 g (2 oz) fresh white breadcrumbs
5 ml (1 tsp) Worcestershire sauce
1 chicken stock cube dissolved in 22.5 ml (1½ tbsp) boiling water
50 g (2 oz) plain flour
2 eggs, lightly beaten
75 g (3 oz) fresh white breadcrumbs
vegetable oil for frying

Mix together the turkey, onion, herbs and apple. Chop for a few seconds in a food processor. Return the mixture to a large bowl and stir in the breadcrumbs, stock and Worcestershire sauce and season to taste. Using your hands, form the mixture into 12 burgers. Dip the burgers in the flour, then in the egg and coat with the breadcrumbs. Heat the vegetable oil in a frying pan and sauté the burgers for about 4 minutes on each side or until golden and cooked through.

Heavenly Barbecued Burgers

These tasty burgers can be made with chicken, beef or lamb – they are irresistible and children love them.

Makes 6 burgers

450 g (1 lb) chopped chicken, minced beef or lamb
1 medium onion, finely chopped
½ red pepper, cored, de-seeded and chopped
15 ml (1 tbsp) vegetable oil
2 tablespoons finely chopped fresh parsley
½ chicken stock cube, dissolved in 45 ml (3 tbsp) of boiling water

25 g (1 oz) breadcrumbs
1 Granny Smith apple, peeled and grated
salt and freshly ground black pepper

Sauce
30 ml (2 tbsp) Hoisin sauce
15 ml (1 tbsp) water
5 ml (1 tsp) sesame oil

Sauté the onion and red pepper until soft (about 10 minutes). Combine these with all the other ingredients and, using your hands, form into about 6 burgers. Mix together the sauce ingredients and brush the burgers with half the sauce. Place the burgers directly on the grill or use a hinged basket, which holds the food between two wire racks. Cook for about 5 minutes on one side. Turn, brush with the remaining sauce and barbecue for 8 to 10 minutes or until cooked through. These can also be cooked under a conventional grill.

Fruity Curried Chicken

A mild, deliciously flavoured chicken curry. This is a recipe that my mother used to make for me when I was a child. I like a pretty tame curry but you can always make it more fiery by using a medium or hot curry powder. Serve with plain rice and poppadums.

Makes 6 portions

1 chicken cut into about 8 pieces
plain flour
salt and freshly ground black pepper
vegetable oil
2 medium onions, peeled and chopped
2 tablespoons mild curry powder
90 ml (6 tbsp) tomato purée
900 ml (1½ pints) chicken stock

1 cooking apple (about 225 g/8 oz), peeled and thinly sliced
1 large carrot, peeled and thinly sliced
2 lemon slices
75 g (3 oz) sultanas
1 bay leaf
1 dessertspoon brown sugar

Pre-heat the oven to 180°C/350°F/Gas 4. Trim any fat from the chicken and remove some of the skin. Coat the chicken with seasoned flour. Fry in the vegetable oil until lightly golden, then drain on kitchen paper and place in a casserole dish. Heat 30 ml (2 tbsp) of vegetable oil in a frying pan and sauté the onion for about 10 minutes or until softened but not coloured. Stir in the curry powder and the tomato purée and continue to cook for 2 to 3 minutes. Stir in 2 tablespoons of flour and stir in 300 ml (½ pint) of the stock.

Add the sliced apple, carrot, lemon slices, sultanas, bay leaf, brown sugar and the rest of the stock. Season with salt and pepper. Pour the sauce over the chicken in the casserole, cover and cook in the oven for 1 hour. Remove the lemon slices and bay leaf, take the chicken off the bone and cut into pieces.

Chicken and Potato Pancake

These pancakes are deliciously thick, golden and crispy with a soft succulent centre. This recipe can be varied by adding other vegetables like grated courgettes or chopped sweet peppers. I make it in a 20 cm (8 in) frying pan and my children enjoy cutting their own slices – it can be eaten either hot or cold.

*Makes 4
portions*

1 chicken breast, cut into pieces, or 75 g
(3 oz) left-over cooked chicken
300 ml (½ pint) chicken or vegetable stock
1 baking potato, peeled and grated
1 onion, peeled and grated

40 g (1½ oz) frozen peas
1 small egg, beaten
1 tablespoon flour
salt and freshly ground black pepper
30 ml (2 tbsp) vegetable oil

Poach the chicken breast in the stock until cooked through (10-15 minutes). Press out the liquid from the grated potato and combine the potato with the onion, frozen peas, egg and flour, and season lightly with some salt and freshly ground black pepper. Dice the chicken and add it to the vegetable mixture.

Heat 15 ml (1 tbsp) of the oil in a 20-cm (8-in) frying pan, tilt the pan so that the oil coats the sides, and press the mixture into the pan. Fry for about 5 minutes or until browned. Turn the pancake on to a plate. Heat the rest of the oil and brown the pancake on the other side for about 7 minutes. Cut into wedges and serve.

Finger Licking Chicken Drumsticks

Chicken drumsticks tend to be very popular with children and are good either hot or cold. This tasty marinade gives them a wonderful flavour and they can be prepared the day before, refrigerated and then wrapped in foil for your child's lunchbox. Always take care to cook chicken right through to avoid food poisoning.

Makes 4 portions

4 large drumsticks

Marinade
22.5 ml (1½ tbsp) cider or white wine vinegar
60 ml (4 tbsp) tomato sauce
30 ml (2 tbsp) clear honey
7.5 ml (½ tbsp) mustard
7.5 ml (½ tbsp) Worcestershire sauce
7.5 ml (½ tbsp) vegetable oil

Mix all the ingredients for the marinade together in a bowl. Skin the drumsticks, make 2 or 3 slashes in the flesh and add to the marinade, turning a few times to make sure that they are well coated. Cover and refrigerate for at least 2 hours or overnight.

Pre-heat the oven to 220°C/425°F/Gas 7. Arrange the drumsticks in a shallow roasting tin and pour over the marinade. Cook for 35-40 minutes, or until cooked through, basting occasionally with the sauce.

Basket-weave Chicken Breasts

The bright orange and green basket-weave pattern made by the carrot and courgette strips looks sensational wrapped around these stuffed chicken breasts. They are surprisingly easy to make and children will love to help weave the vegetable strips together. If your child prefers, you can stuff the chicken breasts with some cheese and ham.

Makes 2 portions

2 large chicken breasts
1 large carrot
1 large courgette
1 shallot, finely chopped
75 g (3 oz) button mushrooms, chopped
7.5 ml (½ tbsp) vegetable oil and a knob of butter
1 teaspoon fresh chopped parsley
a squeeze of lemon juice

1 tablespoon breadcrumbs
salt and freshly ground black pepper

Tarragon sauce
60 ml (2 fl oz) chicken stock
22.5 ml (1½ tbsp) lime or lemon juice
50 g (2 oz) cold butter, cut into cubes
½ tablespoon chopped tarragon
30 ml (2 tbsp) double cream

Using a potato peeler, cut the carrot and courgette lengthways into long thin strips. Blanch them in boiling water for just under 1 minute and place on absorbent kitchen paper to dry.

To prepare the mushroom stuffing, sauté the shallot in the butter and oil until softened, add the chopped mushrooms and cook for 3 to 4 minutes. Add the parsley, lemon juice and breadcrumbs and cook for 2 minutes. Season to taste. Cut a slit in each of the chicken breasts to form a pocket and stuff with the mushroom mixture. Season the chicken.

Place five strips of courgette horizontally quite close together on top of a piece of plastic food wrap (suitable for cooking) just big enough to wrap around the chicken breast. Weave five strips of carrot vertically through the courgette strips to make a basket-weave pattern. Wrap the plastic food wrap and woven vegetables around the chicken breasts to form a parcel. Cook in a steamer for about 20 minutes or until cooked through.

To make the sauce, put the stock and lime or lemon juice in a small saucepan and bring to the boil. Remove from the heat and whisk in the butter. Stir in the tarragon and cream and season to taste. Pour some of the sauce on to a plate, remove the plastic food wrap and place the chicken breasts on top of the sauce.

Chicken Burgers with Courgette and Apple

The grated apples and courgettes give these burgers a lovely moist flavour. They are a great favourite with the whole family and also make a good standby in the freezer.
They are good served in a bun with salad and tomato sauce or simply with baked beans.

***Makes 12
burgers***

*2 breasts of chicken, minced
1 tablespoon fresh chopped parsley
1 onion, finely chopped
2 apples, grated
225 g (8 oz) courgettes, grated
1 chicken stock cube, crumbled*

*salt and freshly ground black pepper
100 g (4 oz) flour
2 eggs, lightly beaten
150 g (5 oz) breadcrumbs
vegetable oil for frying*

Put the chicken, parsley and onion into a food processor and chop for a few seconds on pulse. Squeeze the excess moisture from the apples and courgettes, and mix these into the chicken together with the crumbled stock cube and a little salt and freshly ground black pepper. Using your hands, form into burgers. Coat in flour, then in the beaten egg and then coat with the breadcrumbs. Heat the oil in a large frying pan and sauté the burgers until golden, taking about 6 minutes on each side.

Terrific Turkey Schnitzels

These turkey schnitzels are a great favourite and quick to cook. I like to serve them with spaghettini (very thin spaghetti) and tomato sauce, preferably home-made (see page 56). If you can't find turkey fillets you could substitute chicken breasts pounded quite thin. If you don't have sesame seeds, use 65 g (2½ oz) breadcrumbs instead. It will improve the flavour if you marinate the turkey in lemon juice and garlic before coating with the breadcrumbs and sesame seeds.

***Makes 2
portions***

2 turkey fillets (about 175 g / 6 oz each)

Marinade
*15 ml (1 tbsp) olive oil
30 ml (2 tbsp) lemon juice
1 small clove garlic, thinly sliced*

*plain flour
salt and freshly ground black pepper
1 egg*

*15 ml (1 tbsp) milk
50 g (2 oz) breadcrumbs
2 tablespoons sesame seeds
1 tablespoon finely chopped parsley
1 tablespoon mixed fresh herbs chopped, such
as chives, sage, thyme, rosemary, or
1½ teaspoons dried herbs
15 ml (1 tbsp) vegetable oil
25 g (1 oz) butter*

TIP

You can also use this marinade to marinate chicken breasts, and then cook them under a pre-heated grill or on a griddle with a sprinkling of fresh herbs and some sea salt.

Place the turkey fillets or chicken breasts between sheets of plastic wrap and flatten them with the smooth side of a mallet until very thin. Mix together the ingredients for the marinade and marinate the meat for at least 30 minutes. Remove from the marinade, season the flour with salt and freshly ground black pepper. Lightly beat the egg with the milk.

Mix together the breadcrumbs, sesame seeds, parsley and herbs. Toss each turkey fillet in the seasoned flour, shake off the excess, dip into the egg mixture and roll in the breadcumb mixture. Sauté in a mixture of vegetable oil and butter for about 5 minutes turning halfway through until lightly golden. These taste good with a little fresh lemon juice squeezed over them, so serve with half a lemon if you like.

Nasi Goreng

This is a delicious Indonesian recipe flavoured with peanuts and a mild curry sauce.

Makes 6 portions

2 chicken breasts, diced

Marinade
2 tablespoons soy sauce
½ tablespoon sesame oil
1 tablespoon dark brown sugar

2½ tablespoons vegetable oil
½ tablespoon sesame oil
90g (3½ oz) baby sweetcorn, cut into pieces
1 red pepper, cored, de-seeded and finely chopped

1 large onion, finely chopped
350 g (12 oz) long grain rice
2 teaspoons mild curry powder
½ teaspoon turmeric
900ml (1½ pints) chicken stock
100 g (4 oz) frozen peas
3 spring onions, finely sliced
1 tablespoon molasses or dark brown sugar
50 g (2 oz) roasted peanuts (monkey nuts), finely chopped

Marinate the chicken in the soy sauce, sesame oil and sugar for 30 minutes, then strain the chicken and reserve the marinade. Heat 1 tablespoon of vegetable oil in a wok and stir-fry the chicken for 2 minutes, then set aside. Heat the sesame oil and ½ a tablespoon of vegetable oil and stir-fry the sweetcorn and red pepper for 3 minutes. Heat the remaining 1 tablespoon of vegetable oil in a saucepan and sauté the onion for 3 minutes. Add the rice and cook for 1 minute, stirring to make sure that all the grains are coated. Stir in the curry powder and turmeric and cook for 30 seconds, then add the chicken stock and the reserved marinade from the chicken. Bring to the boil and cook over a high heat for about 6 minutes, then lower the heat and cook for a further 6 minutes, stirring often so that the rice does not stick to the bottom of the pan and burn. Add the frozen peas, spring onions, dark brown sugar, chopped peanuts, cooked vegetables and chicken and cook, stirring, for 2 minutes. Season to taste.

Teddy Bear Chicken Rissoles

The apple brings out a succulent flavour in these chicken rissoles. Shaping them into teddy bear faces is easy and quick and will add oodles of child appeal. (*See photograph, opposite.*)

Makes 6 teddy bears

4 chicken breasts
1 leek, very finely chopped (100 g/4 oz)
1 apple, cored but not peeled and diced
3 or 4 fresh sage leaves, chopped, or 1 teaspoon dried sage
1 x 15 g (½ oz) chicken stock cube, finely crumbled

½ lightly beaten egg
50 g (2 oz) fresh white breadcrumbs
45 ml (3 tbsp) vegetable oil

Decoration
carrot, peas, olives, red pepper, apple

Chop the chicken breasts in a food processor for a few seconds. Transfer the chicken into a mixing bowl and stir in the remaining ingredients, apart from the vegetable oil. Form into 6 teddy bear shapes about 2 cm (¾ in) thick and 9 cm (3½ in) across. Sauté in the vegetable oil for 12 to 15 minutes, turning halfway through, or until golden and cooked through. Decorate with eyes, nose and a mouth.

Easy Yakitori Chicken

In Japan, yakitori bars are popular places to meet, eat and socialise. For extra flavour you can marinate the chicken in the sauce before cooking. You can also add other vegetables like peppers or mushrooms to the skewers if you wish.

Makes 4 skewers

45 ml (3 tbsp) sake or sherry
45 ml (3 tbsp) soy sauce
45 ml (3 tbsp) mirin
1 tablespoon sugar

2 chicken breasts or 8 boned chicken thighs
2 large spring onions or 1 leek, cut into 2.5-cm (1-inch) lengths
15 ml (1 tbsp) vegetable oil

Soak 4 bamboo skewers in water. Put the sake or sherry, soy sauce, mirin and sugar into a small saucepan, bring to the boil and simmer for 6-8 minutes or until syrupy. Cut the chicken breasts into chunks and thread on to the skewers alternately with the spring onion or leek. Stir the vegetable oil into the sauce and brush the chicken liberally with the sauce. Cook under a pre-heated grill for 4 to 5 minutes each side or until the chicken is cooked through.

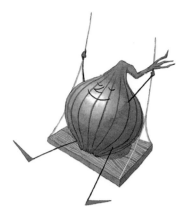

Meat

Meatballs with Sweet and Sour Sauce

These tasty meatballs in a sweet and sour sauce are a family favourite. Red meat provides the best source of iron for you and your child as it is in a form that is absorbed well by the body. Iron deficiency is the most common deficiency in children and will leave your child feeling tired and run-down and make him more prone to infection. It is useful to keep a stock of these meatballs in the freezer.

Makes 5 portions

450 g (1 lb) lean minced beef
1 onion, finely chopped
1 apple, peeled and grated
50 g (2 oz) fresh white breadcrumbs
1 tablespoon chopped fresh parsley
1 chicken stock cube, finely crumbled
30 ml (2 tbsp) cold water
salt and freshly ground black pepper
30 ml (2 tbsp) vegetable oil for frying

Sweet and sour sauce

1 tablespoon soy sauce
½ tablespoon cornflour
1 tablespoon vegetable oil
1 onion, finely chopped
50 g (2 oz) chopped red pepper
1 x 400 g (14 oz) can chopped tomatoes
1 tablespoon malt vinegar
1 teaspoon brown sugar

Mix together all the ingredients for the meatballs apart from the vegetable oil and chop for a few seconds in a food processor. Using floured hands, form into about 20 meatballs. Heat the oil in a frying pan and sauté the meatballs for 10 to 12 minutes, turning occasionally, until browned and sealed.

Meanwhile, to make the sauce, mix together the soy sauce and cornflour in a small bowl. Heat the oil in a pan and sauté the onion for 3 minutes. Add the red pepper and sauté, stirring occasionally, for 2 minutes. Add the tomatoes, vinegar and sugar, season with freshly ground black pepper and simmer for 10 minutes. Add the soy sauce mixture and cook for 2 minutes, stirring occasionally. Blend and sieve or purée the sauce through a mouli.

Pour the sauce over the meatballs, cover and simmer for about 5 minutes or until cooked through.

Annabel's Yummy Burgers

Making your own 'healthy junk food' is one way to encourage fussy eaters to eat better quality food. Adding tomato chutney to burgers gives them a delicious flavour. My children love these. Serve them on their own or in a bun with some salad and maybe a slice of cheese cut into a star.

It's best to freeze burgers uncooked on a tray lined with clingfilm. Then, when frozen, wrap them individually in clingfilm. You can then remove and use as many as you like.

Makes 6 burgers

1 medium red onion, chopped
1 tablespoon sunflower oil
45 g (1¾ oz) carrot, finely chopped
1 garlic clove, crushed
½ teaspoon dried thyme
2 slices white bread
50 g (2 oz) grated apple

250 g (9 oz) minced beef
1 egg yolk
3 tablespoons tomato chutney (I use Waitrose's tomato chutney)
salt and freshly ground black pepper
oil for shallow frying

Sauté the onion in a tablespoon of sunflower oil over a low heat for 6 minutes, then add the carrot and cook for a further 3 minutes. Add the garlic and thyme and cook for 1 minute. Tear the bread into pieces, put in a food processor with the onion mixture and blitz together.

Place the remaining ingredients in a bowl, add the onion mixture, combine well and season to taste. Using flour-dusted hands, form the mixture into 6 burgers.

Fry the burgers in oil for 4–5 minutes each side over a medium-to-low heat. (If you fry over a high heat, because of the sugar in the tomato chutney, the burgers have a tendency to burn.) Alternatively, cook the burgers under a pre-heated grill.

Annabel's Yummy Burgers are shown overleaf

Honeyed Lamb Cutlets

Children like eating food with their fingers, which is one reason why lamb cutlets are popular. They are especially delicious if marinated in honey and soy sauce first.

Makes 6 lamb cutlets

6 lamb cutlets

Marinade
30 ml (2 tbsp) soy sauce
15 ml (1 tbsp) honey
2.5ml (½ tsp) sesame oil

Combine the ingredients for the marinade and marinate the cutlets for at least 2 hours or overnight. Cook under a pre-heated grill for about 8 minutes, turning halfway through. Brush with the marinade during cooking.

Tasty Chinese-style Minced Beef

A lovely combination of tasty minced meat with crunchy water chestnuts. Serve on its own or with rice or noodles. This also makes a delicious filling for tortilla wraps or tacos.

Makes 4 portions

1 tablespoon sesame oil
½ small red pepper
1 onion, chopped
100 g (4 oz) finely chopped courgettes
300 g (11 oz) minced beef

100 g (4 oz) water chestnuts, finely chopped
50–75 g (2–3 oz) baby sweetcorn
75 g (3 oz) beansprouts
2 tablespoons oyster sauce
3 tablespoons rice wine vinegar

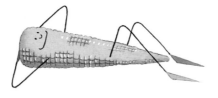
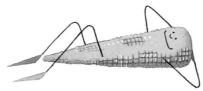

Heat the sesame oil in a wok or frying pan, add the red pepper and onion and cook for 3 minutes. Meanwhile, fry the minced meat in a dry frying pan, stirring to break up with a fork until browned. Add the meat to the wok, stir in the water chestnuts, sweetcorn and beansprouts, cooking for 2-3 minutes. Stir in the oyster sauce and rice wine vinegar and stir-fry for 2 to 3 minutes until slightly thickened.

Lloyd's Leg of Lamb

This is absolutely delicious on a barbecue in summer but also works well in the oven. The lamb is also good eaten cold the next day. Ask your butcher to butterfly a leg of lamb for you – you will end up with a boned, flattened cut of lamb that is easy to carve and takes much less time to cook. This can be served with couscous mixed with some diced roasted vegetables like aubergine, courgette, onion and sweet pepper.

Makes 6 portions

leg of lamb, boned and butterflied

1 teaspoon oregano
60 ml (4 tbsp) lemon juice
2 or 3 garlic cloves, crushed
2 tablespoons chopped parsley
1 teaspoon sea salt
¼ teaspoon ground black pepper

Marinade
150 ml (¼ pint) oil
30 ml (2 tbsp) walnut oil
150 ml (¼ pint) red wine

Mix all the ingredients for the marinade together. Trim away as much excess fat from the lamb as you can. Pierce the lamb all over with the sharp point of a knife and place in a large polythene bag together with the marinade. Tie up the bag and leave in the fridge for 12 to 24 hours, turning frequently until ready to cook.

Barbecue over indirect heat until cooked through. Alternatively, pre-heat the oven to 220°C/425°F/Gas 7. Place the lamb on a rack over a roasting tin and roast in the oven for between 40 minutes and 1 hour depending on its weight and how you like it cooked. Take the lamb out of the oven and let it rest under foil for 15 to 20 minutes before carving across the grain into slices.

Marinated Beef with Vegetables

This delicious quick and easy to prepare beef stir-fry is bound to become a family favourite. It makes a great all-in-one meal.

Makes 4 to 5 portions

225 g (8 oz) beef fillet, rump or sirloin cut into strips

Marinade
15 ml (1 tbsp) soy sauce
15 ml (1 tbsp) sake or sherry
5 ml (1 tsp) sesame oil
1 teaspoon cornflour

175 g (6 oz) pasta twirls
45 ml (3 tbsp) sunflower oil
1 clove garlic, crushed
1 onion, thinly sliced
100 g (4 oz) carrots, sliced or cut into stars

175 g (6 oz) new potatoes
100 g (4 oz) French beans, topped and tailed
100 g (4 oz) red pepper, cut into strips
salt and freshly ground black pepper

Sauce
½ chicken stock cube dissolved in 90 ml (6 tbsp) boiling water
2.5 ml (½ tsp) rice wine vinegar
5 ml (1 tsp) soy sauce
1 teaspoon sugar
½ teaspoon cornflour

TIP
You can marinade foods in plastic bags instead of bowls that you have to wash up. Be sure you flip the bag from time to time to make sure everything gets a good soak.

Mix together the ingredients for the marinade and marinate the beef strips for at least 20 minutes. Cook the pasta in a large pan of lightly salted boiling water according to the instructions on the packet, drain, set aside and keep warm. Steam the carrots, potatoes and French beans for about 6 minutes or until tender.

Meanwhile, heat 15 ml (1 tbsp) of the vegetable oil in a wok or frying pan and stir-fry the beef for 3 minutes. Take out the beef and set aside. In the same pan, heat the remaining oil and sauté the garlic and onion for 3 minutes. Mix together all the ingredients for the sauce. Add the red pepper to the onion and cook for 2 minutes, cut the potatoes into slices and add these together with the carrots, French beans and beef and season with some salt and freshly ground black pepper. Stir in the sauce and cooked pasta and cook for 2 minutes.

Marinated Beef Skewers

Marinating cubes of beef in this sauce gives them a delicious flavour and also tenderises the meat. This is a particular favourite of my three children. If you prefer, you can make these skewers very successfully without the vegetables.

***Makes 3 to 4
portions***

12 oz fillet steak cut into cubes

Marinade
12 mm (½ in) ginger root, grated
1 clove garlic, crushed
15 ml (1 tbsp) dark soy sauce
5 ml (1 tsp) rice wine vinegar

15 ml (1 tbsp) vegetable oil
15 ml (1 tbsp) honey
½ red pepper, cut into chunks
1 small onion, cut into chunks
4 button mushrooms
vegetable oil

Mix together all the ingredients for the marinade and marinate the cubes of beef for at least 1 hour. Toss the red pepper, onion and mushrooms in a little vegetable oil and thread on to the skewers alternately with the cubes of beef. Place on aluminium foil in a grill pan and grill for 3 to 4 minutes each side under a medium grill.

Maria's Luscious Lamb

Maria is a fabulous Portuguese cook and this is one of her specialities. This cut of lamb cooked on the bone is full of flavour and is very tender. For children it's best to remove the lamb from the bone, but for adults one small-sized shank each is ideal.

***Makes 2
portions***

2 shanks of lamb
2 shallots, chopped
1 teaspoon ground cumin
½ teaspoon turmeric
1 teaspoon paprika
½ teaspoon cayenne pepper

salt
30 ml (2 tbsp) olive oil
½ glass white wine (optional)
*200 ml (6½ fl oz) stock (lamb, chicken or
vegetable)*
1 bay leaf

Sprinkle the shallots and spices over the lamb, season with a little salt and pour over the olive oil. Leave to marinate for a few hours. Pre-heat the oven to 160°C/325°F/Gas 3. Brown the lamb well in a large casserole on a stove or cook in a hot oven in a roasting tin until browned. Add the wine, stock and bay leaf. Cover the casserole or cover the roasting tin with foil and cook in the oven for 1½ hours for small shanks or 2 hours for larger, until tender.

Sesame Beef Stir-fry

Provided you are not vegetarian, it is important to include red meat in your child's diet, as red meat provides the richest source of iron and iron deficiency is the most common nutritional deficiency in children in the UK. This recipe is a firm family favourite in my house. I usually make it using tail fillet cut into thin strips, which is slightly cheaper but has exactly the same taste and soft texture of proper fillet steak. *(See photograph, page 88.)*

Makes 4 portions

1 tablespoon sesame oil
1 clove garlic, crushed
1 medium carrot, cut into matchsticks
100 g (4 oz) baby sweetcorn, cut into quarters
1 courgette (approx. 100 g/4 oz), cut into matchsticks
300 g (10 oz) beef fillet, or rump steak, cut into very fine strips

1 tablespoon cornflour
150 ml (5 fl oz) beef stock
2 tablespoons dark brown sugar
2 tablespoons soy sauce
a few drops Tabasco sauce
1 tablespoon sesame seeds

Heat the sesame oil in a wok and stir-fry the garlic, carrots, sweetcorn and courgette for 3 to 4 minutes. Add the beef and continue to stir-fry for 4 to 5 minutes. Mix the cornflour together with 1 tablespoon of water and stir into the beef stock. Stir this into the pan together with the sugar, soy sauce, Tabasco and sesame seeds. Bring to the simmer, cook until slightly thickened and serve with rice.

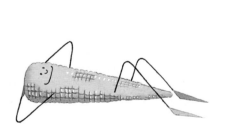

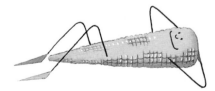

Nicholas's Multi-layered Cottage Pie

A rather luxurious version of an old-fashioned favourite comfort food. You can either make one large cottage pie or several individual portions in ramekin dishes so that you can freeze some portions for use later. It looks especially good in a Pyrex dish so you can see the colourful layers. If you prefer, you could make an ordinary cottage pie – simply leave out the layers of vegetables.
My son Nicholas is a big meat eater and can easily eat three huge platefuls of this for his supper!

Makes 6 portions

450 g carrots, peeled and chopped
a generous knob of butter

2½ tablespoons vegetable oil
450 g (1 lb) minced beef
1 large onion, finely chopped
100 g (4 oz) leek, finely chopped
100 g (4 oz) red pepper, finely chopped
1 garlic clove, crushed
150 g (5 oz) button mushrooms, sliced
1 x 400 g (14 oz) can of chopped tomatoes, drained
1 tablespoon tomato purée

2 teaspoons Worcestershire sauce
½ teaspoon dried mixed herbs
1 beef stock cube dissolved in 300 ml (½ pint) boiling water
salt and freshly ground black pepper

675 g (1 lb 4 oz) potatoes, peeled and cut into chunks
50 g (2 oz) unsalted butter
6 tablespoons milk
salt and a little white pepper
200 g (7 oz) frozen peas
1 beaten egg

Cook the carrots in boiling lightly salted water for 20 minutes or until tender, then mash with the butter until smooth.

Heat half a tablespoon of the oil in a large non-stick frying pan and sauté the beef for 7–8 minutes or until all the liquid has evaporated. Remove the beef from the pan and set aside.

Heat the remaining oil in a large casserole and sauté the onion and leek for 5 minutes. Add the red pepper and sauté for 3 minutes, then add the garlic and sauté for 30 seconds. Add the mushrooms and sauté for 2 minutes. Add the tomato purée, tomatoes, Worcestershire sauce, herbs and beef stock, and simmer for about 30 minutes. Season to taste.

Meanwhile, boil the potatoes for 15–20 minutes, then drain. Return the cooked potatoes to the empty saucepan and mash together with the butter, milk, salt and pepper until smooth.

Place the mashed carrots in the base of a glass ovenproof dish or use mini dishes to make individual portions. Arrange the meat on top, then cover with a layer of cooked peas and top with a layer of potato. Brush the potato with the beaten egg and cook under a pre-heated grill for 6–7 minutes or until the top is browned.

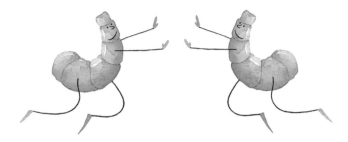

Fish

Very Easy Florentine Fillets

Fillets of tender white fish on a bed of fresh spinach covered with cheese sauce is a classic and favourite combination.

Makes 2 portions

❄

225 g (8 oz) fresh spinach or 100 g (4 oz) frozen spinach
25 g (1 oz) butter
125 ml (4 fl oz) double cream
25 g (1 oz) Parmesan cheese, grated

225 g (8 oz) fillet of cod or haddock, filleted and skinned
15 ml (1 tbsp) milk
salt and freshly ground black pepper
20 g (¾ oz) Gruyère or Cheddar cheese, grated

Wash the spinach and remove any tough stalks. Cook in a saucepan with just a little water clinging to the leaves until wilted. Squeeze out any excess moisture. Melt half the butter and sauté the spinach for 1 minute and season to taste. (Alternatively, the spinach can be cooked in a microwave.)

Meanwhile, put the double cream, remaining butter and Parmesan cheese in a small saucepan and heat gently until the butter has melted. Lightly season the fish, put into a suitable container, dot with butter and pour over the milk. Cook in a microwave on high for about 4 minutes or until the fish flakes easily with a fork. (Alternatively, the fish can be cooked under the grill.)

Pour the cooking liquid from the fish into the cheese sauce. Arrange the spinach on a greased oven-proof dish and place the fish fillets on top. Pour over the cheese sauce and sprinkle with the grated Gruyère or Cheddar cheese. Brown under a pre-heated grill for 2 to 3 minutes.

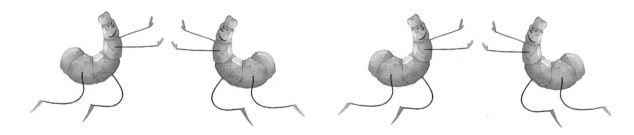

Tasty 10-minute Prawn Stir-fry

Here is a tasty stir-fry with colourful crunchy vegetables and carrot curls which is very quick to prepare. It is good served with Perfect Chinese Fried Rice (see page 134).

Makes 4 portions

100 g (4 oz) baby sweetcorn
100 g (4 oz) carrots
22.5 ml (1½ tbsp) vegetable oil
2 spring onions
100 g (4 oz) sugar snap peas or mangetout

250 ml (8 fl oz) chicken stock
15 ml (1 tbsp) soy sauce
30 ml (2 tbsp) sake or sherry
2 tablespoons cornflour
225 g (8 oz) cooked king prawns

Halve the sweetcorn lengthways, then cut across in half again. Using a potato peeler, cut thin strips from the carrot and cut these in half again to make long, thin, curly strips of carrot. Heat the oil in a wok or frying pan and sauté the spring onion for 1 minute. Add the other vegetables and stir-fry for 2 to 3 minutes. Remove the vegetables and set aside. Mix together the chicken stock, soy sauce, sake or sherry and cornflour. Pour the mixture into the wok and stir constantly while bringing to the boil. Reduce the heat and simmer, stirring, for 1 to 2 minutes until thickened. Stir in the prawns and the vegetables and heat through.

Teriyaki Glazed Trout Fillets

Oily fish like salmon, trout, tuna and mackerel contain omega-3 fatty acids that help to reduce the risk of heart disease and strokes, as well as being important for brain development.

Makes 2 portions

4 trout fillets

Marinade
30 ml (2 tbsp) soy sauce
30 ml (2 tbsp) sake or sherry
30 ml (2 tbsp) mirin

Mix together all the ingredients for the marinade in a small saucepan and bring to the boil. Simmer for 2 to 3 minutes. Arrange the trout fillets in a shallow dish and pour over the hot marinade. Set aside for about 15 minutes. Heat the grill and lay the fillets on a grill pan lined with foil and grill for 5 to 6 minutes on the fleshy side, until cooked. Pour over the sauce.

King Prawn Stir-fry with Sugar Snap Peas

Stir-fries make popular, quick and easy meals for the whole family, especially if you have a quantity of chicken stock ready prepared and in the freezer. This particular recipe could also be made with fresh uncooked prawns.

Makes 4 portions

300 g (10 oz) cooked king prawns (de-veined)

100 g (4 oz) button mushrooms, cut in half
150 g (5 oz) sugar snap peas

Marinade
1 egg white, lightly beaten
1 teaspoon cornflour
a pinch of salt
a pinch of ground white pepper

45 ml (3 tbsp) vegetable oil
2 eggs, lightly beaten
1 clove garlic, crushed
1 onion, thinly sliced
100 g (4 oz) baby corn, cut in half

Sauce
375 ml (12 fl oz) chicken stock
15 ml (1 tbsp) soy sauce
15 ml (1 tbsp) sesame oil
1½ tablespoons caster sugar
7.5 ml (½ tbsp) cider vinegar
1½ tablespoons cornflour
2 spring onions, finely sliced
a little ground white pepper

Mix together the beaten egg white, cornflour and seasoning and marinate the prawns in this mixture for about 10 minutes. To make the sauce, mix together the stock, soy sauce, sesame oil, sugar and vinegar. In a small bowl mix 45 ml (3 tbsp) of the sauce with the cornflour until smooth and then stir this into the rest of the sauce. Pour the sauce into a saucepan, bring to the boil and then simmer, stirring, for 2 to 3 minutes until thickened. Stir in the spring onions and season with the white pepper.

Strain the marinade from the prawns and discard. Heat 15 ml (1 tbsp) of the oil in a frying pan and sauté the prawns for about 2 minutes then set aside. Heat another tablespoon of oil in the pan and swirl the beaten egg around to form a thin layer and cook until set. Remove from the pan and fold it over three times like a swiss roll, cut into strips and set aside.

Add the remaining oil to the pan and sauté the garlic and onion for 2 minutes. Stir-fry the corn, button mushrooms and sugar snap peas for 6 minutes. Add the prawns and the sauce and cook for 2 minutes or until heated through.

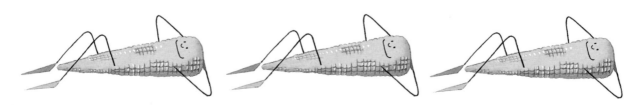

Yummy Fish in Orange Sauce

This is a great way to cook up a fillet of fresh fish in just a few minutes. As it is so easy, I make it for my own lunch sometimes. For more people, simply increase the quantities.

Makes 1 portion

1 x 225g (8 oz) fillet of cod, haddock or hake, skinned
plain flour
salt and freshly ground black pepper

20 g (¾ oz) butter
5 ml (1 tsp) soy sauce
5 ml (1 tsp) freshly squeezed orange juice

Season some flour with a little salt and freshly ground black pepper and coat the fish in the seasoned flour. Melt the butter in a frying pan and sauté the fish for about 5 minutes, turning occasionally. Mix together the soy sauce and orange juice, pour over the fish, turn up the heat and cook for about 1 minute.

Mermaid Morsels

These miniature fish balls are very tasty. You can use any combination of white fish available, such as cod, haddock, whiting, hake or halibut. A fishmonger should be able to prepare it for you. They are good served hot or cold.

Makes 20 balls

450 g (1 lb) minced or finely chopped mixed white fish
1 large onion, finely chopped
15 ml (1 tbsp) vegetable oil and a knob of butter plus extra for frying the fish balls
1 carrot, finely grated
1 tablespoon finely chopped fresh parsley

1 egg, lightly beaten
2 dessertspoons sugar
1 teaspoon salt
a little freshly ground black pepper
22.5 ml (1½ tbsp) cold water
2 tablespoons flour plus extra for coating the fish balls

Fry the onion in a mixture of oil and butter until soft and lightly golden. Combine the minced fish, fried onion, carrot and parsley. Beat the egg together with the sugar, salt and pepper until frothy and add the egg mixture to the minced fish. Finally, mix in the cold water and 2 tablespoons of the flour. Using your hands, form into small walnut-sized balls, roll in flour and fry in a mixture of vegetable oil and butter until golden, turning occasionally.

Spaghetti Marinara

It's very important that you only buy very fresh seafood, so always buy it from a reputable source. This is a delicious pasta sauce and you can make it quite spicy for adults by adding more chilli if you like. I would not recommend giving seafood to very young children.

Makes 4 portions

900 g (2 lb) mussels
8 large raw prawns
350 g (12 oz) spaghetti

Sauce
30 ml (2 tbsp) olive oil
4 shallots, finely chopped

1 clove garlic, crushed
2 tablespoons chopped fresh parsley
6 tablespoons dry white wine
800 g (1 lb 12 oz) can of chopped tomatoes
1 or 2 dried red chillies, crushed, or a good pinch of red pepper flakes
salt and freshly ground black pepper

Discard any mussels that are not closed, then scrub well under cold water and pull off and discard the beards. Set the mussels aside. Peel, de-vein and cut the prawns in half lengthways. Cook the spaghetti in a large pan of lightly salted water according to the instructions on the packet.

Heat the olive oil in a frying pan and sauté the shallots and garlic for 2 minutes, add the parsley and sauté for 1 minute. Add the wine, simmer for 2 minutes, then add the tomatoes and chilli(es) and simmer for 4 minutes. Add the mussels and cook for 4 to 5 minutes. Discard any mussels that do not open. Add the prawns, simmer for about 2 minutes and season to taste.

Drain the spaghetti, return to the warm pan, add the marinara sauce and toss gently. If you like, remove the mussels from their shells (discard any where the shells have not opened) and mix with the spaghetti.

Simply Super Salmon Teriyaki

Oily fish like salmon, trout, tuna and mackerel contain omega-3 fatty acids which protect against heart disease and strokes. The old wives' tale that fish is good for the brain is therefore true, as omega-3 essential fats optimise messaging between nerve cells in the brain. This is vital for proper brain functioning and research suggests that a diet rich in omega-3 fats can also improve the performance of children who suffer attention defect syndrome or are dyspraxic. My children and I all love Japanese food and it is well worth investing in bottles of sake and mirin (a sweet Japanese cooking wine) as you will want to make this recipe over and over again. Serve with basmati rice.

Makes 4 portions

4 x 150 g (5 oz) thick fillets of salmon, skinned

30 ml (2 tbsp) vegetable oil
150 g (5 oz) button mushrooms, sliced
150 g (5 oz) beansprouts

Marinade
80 ml (3 fl oz) soy sauce
100 ml (4 fl oz) sake
50 ml (2 fl oz) mirin (sweet sake for cooking)
2 tablespoons sugar

Mix the ingredients for the marinade together in a saucepan and stir over a medium heat until the sugar has dissolved. Marinate the salmon in the sauce for 10 minutes.

Heat half the oil and sauté the mushrooms for 2 minutes, then add the beansprouts and cook for 2 minutes more. Meanwhile, drain the salmon, reserving the marinade. Heat the remaining oil in a frying pan and sauté the salmon for 1 or 2 minutes on each side or until slightly browned. Pour away the excess oil from the frying pan. Alternatively, it is particularly good if you cook the salmon on a very hot griddle pan brushed with a little oil.

Whichever method you choose, after 2 minutes pour a little of the teriyaki marinade over the salmon and continue to cook for a few minutes, basting occasionally. Simmer the remaining marinade in a small saucepan until thickened. Divide the vegetables between four plates, place the salmon on top and pour the teriyaki sauce over the fish.

Fishing for Compliments

It's a shame that for many children the only fish that they enjoy eating is fish fingers. However, this is a very tasty fish recipe that I have invented for children although it's also delicious for the whole family and may well tempt even the most reluctant fish eater.

Makes 2 portions

❄

Sauce
250 ml (8 fl oz) chicken stock
10 ml (2 tsp) soy sauce
5 ml (1 tsp) sesame oil
1 tablespoon sugar
5 ml (1 tsp) cider vinegar
1 tablespoon cornflour
1 spring onion, finely sliced

350 g (12 oz) plaice, sole or cod fillets
skinned and cut into strips about 6.5 cm
(2½ in) long
15 ml (1 tbsp) lemon juice
15 ml (1 tbsp) water
1 tablespoon chopped onion
45 ml (3 tbsp) vegetable oil
100 g (4 oz) courgettes, cut into strips
50 g (2 oz) red pepper, cut into strips
plain flour
salt and freshly ground black pepper

Rinse the fish fillets and pat dry with paper towels. Mix together the lemon juice, water and chopped onion and marinate the fish in this mixture for about 30 minutes.

To make the sauce, mix together the stock, soy sauce, sesame oil, sugar, vinegar and cornflour. Pour the sauce into a saucepan, bring to the boil and then simmer, stirring, for 2 to 3 minutes until thickened and smooth. Stir in the spring onion.

Heat 15 ml (1 tbsp) of the vegetable oil in a pan and sauté the courgette and red pepper for 4 minutes. Strain the marinade from the fish and discard (including the onion), coat the fish lightly in seasoned flour. Heat the remaining oil in a pan and sauté the fish for about 3 minutes each side or until cooked. Add the vegetables, pour over the sauce and cook for 2 minutes.

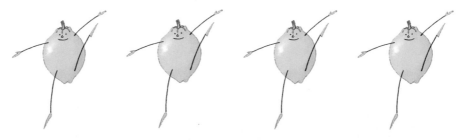

Mini Fish Pies

If you want your child to grow up liking fish then you should try these delicious mini fish pies. It is nice to make individual portions for your child in ramekin dishes – much more appealing than a dollop of fish pie on a plate. You can store extra portions in the freezer for days when you don't want to cook. Before serving you can decorate them with faces made from vegetables and herbs if you like. *(See photograph, page 102.)*

Makes 4 mini fish pies

Mashed potato
1 kg (2 lb) potatoes, peeled and chopped
40 g (1½ oz) butter
4 tablespoons milk
salt and white pepper
1 egg, beaten

250 g (8½ oz) salmon fillet, skinned
250 g (8½ oz) cod fillet, skinned
1 bay leaf

1 sprig parsley
6 peppercorns
500 ml (1 pint) milk
25 g (1 oz) butter
1 onion, peeled and finely chopped
3 tablespoons plain flour
40 g (1½ oz) Cheddar cheese, grated
salt and freshly ground black pepper
125 g (4 oz) frozen peas

Pre-heat the oven to 180°C/350°F/Gas 4. For the mashed potato, boil some lightly salted water, add the potatoes and boil until tender. Meanwhile, put the salmon and cod in a shallow pan with the bay leaf, parsley, peppercorns and milk. Bring to the boil then reduce the heat. Cover and simmer for 5 minutes or until the fish flakes easily. Remove the fish, strain the milk and reserve. Flake the fish with a fork, checking carefully for bones, and set aside. Remove the peppercorns, bay leaf and parsley.

Melt the butter in a saucepan, add the onion and sauté until softened (about 3 to 4 minutes). Stir in the flour to make a paste and cook for 1 minute. Gradually add the strained milk, stirring until the sauce thickens. Remove from the heat and stir in the grated cheese until melted. Season to taste, then stir in the frozen peas. Spoon the fish into four ramekin dishes.

Drain and mash the potatoes. Add the butter, milk and seasoning. Spread the potato over the fish in the ramekin dishes, making lines on the surface using a fork. Brush with beaten egg.

Place in the pre-heated oven for 15 to 20 minutes and finish off under a pre-heated grill until browned. Decorate with faces made from vegetables if liked (see page 102).

Posh Fish Fingers

Crushed cornflakes make a delicious coating for fried fish. Serve with oven-baked chips and maybe wrap them up in a newspaper or a comic for fun. My children like fish and chips sprinkled with a little malt vinegar.

Makes 4 portions

450 g (1 lb) cod, haddock, plaice or hake fillets, skinned
salt and freshly ground black pepper
50 g (2 oz) plain flour

1 egg, lightly beaten
50 g (2 oz) cornflakes
1 tablespoon fresh chopped parsley
vegetable oil for frying

Put the fish into four portions and season. Coat in flour and then dip into the beaten egg. Crush the cornflakes (this can be done by putting them in a bag and crushing them with a rolling pin) and mix with the chopped parsley. Roll the fish fillets into the cornflake mixture to coat and fry in vegetable oil until golden and cooked through.

Perfect Paella

This paella is simple and quick to prepare. It is very important that you use only fresh live mussels and any uncooked mussels that are already open should be discarded. Once the mussels are cooked the shells should open, but do not eat cooked mussels if the shells remain closed. You can sometimes buy bags of frozen or fresh mixed seafood, which could also be used for this recipe and then you may find that the mussels are already cooked and out of their shells. *(See photograph, overleaf.)*

Makes 4 portions

1 clove garlic, crushed
1 onion, chopped
15 ml (1 tbsp) olive oil
1 red pepper, cut into strips
300 g (10 oz) easy cook rice
1 teaspoon turmeric
1 teaspoon mild chilli powder

1.2 litres (2 pints) chicken stock
1 bay leaf
2 tablespoons chopped fresh parsley
150 g (5 oz) fresh prawns
225 g (8 oz) fresh clams
350 g (12 oz) mussels
100 g (4 oz) frozen peas

Sauté the onion and garlic in the oil for 1 minute. Add the red pepper and cook for another 3 minutes. Add the rice and the turmeric and chilli powder and stir in the pan for about 1 minute. Pour in the stock, add the bay leaf and cook for 15 minutes over a medium heat. Add the parsley and cook for about 5 minutes. Turn the heat up, add the fish and frozen peas and cook for 1 to 2 minutes over a high heat. Reduce the heat and cover and cook for about 5 minutes or until the fish is cooked. Remove any shells that haven't opened.

Evelyn's Tasty Fish Pie

This is one of the recipes that my mother used to make and I remember how much I enjoyed eating it as a child. Now I make it for my children.

Makes 4 to 5 portions

450 g (1 lb) fillets cod or haddock, skinned
plain flour
salt and freshly ground black pepper
1 egg, beaten
100 g (4 oz) fine breadcrumbs
vegetable oil
1 onion, finely chopped
15 ml (1 tbsp) olive oil
100 g (4 oz) green pepper, cored, de-seeded and chopped
150 g (5 oz) red pepper, cored, de-seeded and chopped

1 x 400 g (14 oz) can of chopped tomatoes
30 ml (2 tbsp) tomato purée
1 tablespoon chopped fresh parsley

Cheese sauce
25 g (1 oz) butter
25 g (1 oz) plain flour
250 ml (8 fl oz) milk
75 g (3 oz) Cheddar cheese, grated
40 g (1½ oz) Parmesan cheese, grated

Pre-heat the oven to 180°C/350°F/Gas 4. Cut the fillets of fish into about eight pieces. Dip each fillet into seasoned flour, then into the lightly beaten egg and finally coat in breadcrumbs. Sauté in the oil until golden on both sides and then drain on kitchen paper.

Sauté the onion in the olive oil for 2 to 3 minutes, add the peppers and continue to cook for 5 minutes. Drain the juice from the tomatoes and add the chopped tomatoes to the peppers together with the tomato purée. Cook for 5 minutes. Season to taste and sprinkle with the parsley. Mix the cooked fish with the tomato sauce.

To make the cheese sauce, melt the butter, stir in the flour and cook for 1 minute over a low heat to make a roux. Gradually whisk in the milk, stirring, over a medium heat until thickened. Bring to the boil and then cook for 1 minute. Remove from the heat and stir in two-thirds of the Cheddar and Parmesan cheese, reserving the remainder for sprinkling over the top of the fish pie.

Put the fish in tomato sauce into an oven-proof dish, cover with the cheese sauce and sprinkle the remaining cheese on top. Cook in the oven for 20 minutes. Brown the top under a pre-heated grill for a few minutes to finish off.

Soupa Tuna Tagliatelle

This is a tasty and nutritious pasta dish that is quick and easy to make for the whole family using store cupboard ingredients, including a can of tomato soup.

Makes 6 portions

225 g (8 oz) green and white tagliatelle
25 g (1 oz) butter
1 small onion, finely chopped
1 heaped tablespoon cornflour
1 x 405 g (14 oz) can of cream
of tomato soup
2 tablespoons chopped fresh parsley
½ teaspoon dried mixed herbs
1 x 400 g (14 oz) can of tuna

Cheese sauce
25 g (1 oz) butter

20 g (¾ oz) flour
375 ml (12 fl oz) milk
a pinch of dried mustard powder
100 g (4 oz) Cheddar cheese, grated
1 tablespoon snipped chives
50 g (2 oz) sweetcorn, cooked
salt and freshly ground black pepper

Topping
25 g (1 oz) brown breadcrumbs
25 g (1 oz) Cheddar cheese, grated
1 tablespoon freshly grated Parmesan cheese

Pre-heat the oven to 180°C/350°F/Gas 4. Cook the tagliatelle in a large saucepan of lightly salted boiling water until just tender. Melt the butter in a saucepan and sauté the onion until softened. Mix the cornflour with 30 ml (2 tbsp) cold water until dissolved. Mix the cornflour mixture, tomato soup, parsley and herbs with the sautéed onion and cook over a medium heat for about 5 minutes or until the sauce has thickened. Stir the tuna fish into the sauce and mix with the cooked tagliatelle.

To make the cheese sauce, put the butter, flour and milk into a saucepan and cook over a medium heat. Using a balloon whisk, keep whisking the mixture until it boils and thickens to form a smooth sauce. Add the mustard powder and simmer for 2 to 3 minutes. Remove from the heat and stir in 75 g (3 oz) of the cheese until melted. Stir in the chives and cooked sweetcorn and season to taste.

Arrange the tuna and pasta mixture in a 25 x 20 cm (10 x 8 in) oven-proof dish and pour over the cheese sauce. Mix together the breadcrumbs and grated cheeses and scatter these over the top. Cook in the oven for 20 minutes. Brown under a hot grill for a few minutes before serving.

Chinese Noodles with Prawns and Beansprouts

This noodle dish is quick and easy to prepare and very versatile. You can use shredded chicken or pork instead of the prawns or perhaps strips of omelette if you are vegetarian. You can also substitute other vegetables like strips of courgette, carrot or baby sweetcorn. This makes a good accompaniment to stir-fries.

Makes 4 portions

175 g (6 oz) medium egg noodles
30 ml (2 tbsp) vegetable oil
4 spring onions, sliced
½ to 1 teaspoon finely chopped red chilli
(optional)
1 clove garlic, crushed
1 tablespoon fresh chopped parsley
100 g (4 oz) button, oyster or shitake

mushrooms, sliced
100 g (4 oz) large cooked peeled prawns
45 ml (3 tbsp) oyster sauce
1 teaspoon caster sugar
125 ml (4 fl oz) water
100 g (4 oz) fresh beansprouts
125 ml (4 fl oz) chicken stock

Drop the noodles into a large pan of boiling water. Return to the boil and simmer for 4 minutes. Drain and set aside. One more line needed to fill here.

Meanwhile, heat the vegetable oil in a wok or frying pan and stir-fry the spring onions, chilli (if using), garlic and parsley for 1 minute. Add the mushrooms and prawns and stir-fry for 2 minutes. Add the oyster sauce, caster sugar and water. Stir in the beansprouts and stock and cook for 2 minutes. Return the noodles to the pan and heat through.

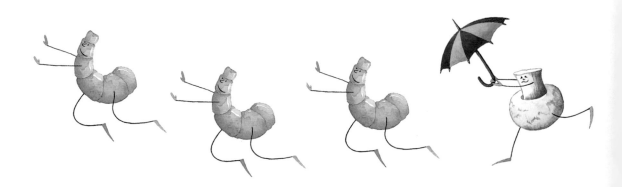

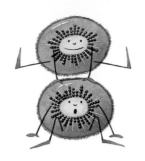

Low-fat
Recipes

Low-fat Recipes

Shocking new figures show that one in six 10-year-olds is classed as obese and by the time they reach 15, the figure is almost one in five. Obesity in British children has doubled in the last 20 years but it's no surprise when today's children not only eat more junk food but are also becoming less and less active.

Children who are overweight face a greater risk of developing a serious illness such as heart disease, diabetes or cancer, and more people are dying in Britain due to being overweight or obese than anywhere else in Europe. Children as young as 8 are showing signs of heart disease and 10-year-olds are developing the type of diabetes once found only in adults. Around one in eleven deaths is now linked to carrying excess fat and is being blamed on the rise of aggressively marketed fat-laden foods and couch-potato lifestyles. Overweight children suffer both physically and emotionally and those who remain heavy in adolescence tend to stay that way into adulthood.

FOODS TO AVOID

Fast food, pre-prepared meals and sugary, fizzy drinks are high in calories, fats, salt and sugar but low in essential nutrients. Sadly, most children eat less than half the recommended five portions of fruit and vegetables a day. However, children now consume 30 times more soft drinks and 5 times more confectionery than they did in 1950. Portion sizes are ballooning too: most snacks and sweets are sold in 'super size' for just a few pennies more than standard size. It's important to cut out as much processed junk food from your child's diet as you can, as these are the foods that are high in saturated fat, salt and sugar.

The types of carbohydrate you give your child affect their energy level, their ability to concentrate and their appetite. Complex carbohydrates like wholegrain bread, porridge, potatoes and pasta get broken down into sugar in the blood, slowly providing a steady supply of energy. On the other hand, foods like refined sugary breakfast cereals, white bread and jam and chocolate biscuits are broken down quickly, rapidly increasing the level of sugar in the blood. This gives a quick burst of energy followed by a drop in sugar levels, leaving a child tired, unable to concentrate and hungry.

Over half the children in this country eat twice as much salt as they should and it is estimated that by reducing the amount of salt we eat, 14% fewer people would suffer strokes and 10% fewer people would suffer a heart attack. About three quarters of the salt children consume comes from processed foods, so, to reduce your child's salt intake you must limit the amount of processed foods, snack and fast foods such as pizzas, chicken nuggets, spaghetti hoops and crisps that your child eats.

HOW TO LOSE WEIGHT

By adopting a healthier diet, a child's weight gain should keep apace of his increasing height. Rather than restrict food, you should change the type of food that you give your child and the way you cook it. Give more fruit and vegetables and grill or bake rather than fry foods.

Remember that fitness is vital too: make exercise fun by buying a trampoline or climbing frame for the garden, or get involved yourself with ball games or family bike rides. Encourage your child to walk or cycle to school if possible, or take the dog for walks in the park.

Avoid using the term 'diet' or children can end up with eating disorders. What you need to do is to stabilise a child's weight while they grow. The message should be that you want your child to be healthier rather than slimmer.

Many parents who work full time think that cooking fresh food is too time-consuming, but it doesn't have to be. Opposite are some suggestions for healthy alternatives.

ENCOURAGING CHILDREN TO LOSE WEIGHT

✓ It is not good for your child to go to school on an empty stomach. Try to give your child a high-fibre cereal like Weetabix, Porridge or Shredded Wheat with skimmed milk and some fresh fruit. Boiled or poached eggs with wholemeal toast are good too.

✓ When children come home from school they are usually starving. Have some fresh fruit cut up into pieces or raw vegetable sticks and cherry tomatoes with a tasty dip. Leave snacks like these on a low shelf in the fridge where children can help themselves.

✓ Char-grilling food on a ridged pan is a tasty way to prepare chicken, fish and meat and uses minimal oil.

✓ Instead of chips offer high-fibre jacket potatoes. If going for chips choose low-fat oven chips; the thick-cut variety absorb less oil.

✓ If vegetables are not popular try a new approach, e.g. stir-fries with soy sauce and noodles; blend vegetables into a tomato sauce for pasta; make a tomato soup with fresh tomatoes, onion and carrots; or find a salad dressing that your child really likes.

✓ Try to include as much fruit as possible: add fruit to breakfast cereals, or make fruit smoothies combinations like peach, banana and strawberry. Desserts like cakes or sponge-based puddings should be a treat rather than the norm. For variety, present fruit in different ways; for example, serve kiwi fruit in an egg cup. You can also make delicious ice lollies by puréeing fruit and mixing it with pure fruit juice.

✓ Give more complex carbohydrates like baked potatoes, muesli or porridge, wholemeal bread and vegetables. These are absorbed more slowly into the bloodstream than simple carbohydrates like white rice, sugary refined breakfast cereals, cakes and biscuits, thus providing a more constant supply of energy.

✓ Give healthy snacks: Popcorn, Twiglets or Rice Cakes are a good alternative to crisps. Instead of biscuits or chocolate bars, give healthy snacks like pitta bread filled with tuna or chicken salad. Pumpkin or sunflower seeds sprinkled with a little soy sauce and honey and baked under a grill for a few minutes make a nutritious, tasty snack.

✓ Cut down on sugary drinks but be careful about substituting fruit juices; they may be healthier but they also contain high levels of sugar. Encourage your child to drink water.

✓ Cut out between meal snacks like crisps or chocolate biscuits and give healthy foods instead like fresh fruit or raw vegetables and a dip.

✓ Don't buy foods that you don't want your child to eat. In a house where there is only fruit for dessert your child is more likely to eat fruit if there isn't chocolate cake in the fridge.

Penne with Tuna and Tomato Sauce

Pasta is a good source of complex carbohydrates, which provide long-lasting energy. The red onion and sunblush tomatoes give this pasta dish a lovely flavour.

Makes 4 portions

200 g (7 oz) penne
2 tablespoons light olive oil
1 red onion, peeled and sliced
4 plum tomatoes, quartered, de-seeded and roughly chopped

200 g (7 oz) tin tuna in oil (drained)
75 g (3 oz) sunblush tomatoes, chopped
1 tablespoon balsamic vinegar
small handful basil leaves, torn
salt and pepper

Cook the penne in lightly salted boiling water according to the packet instructions. Heat the olive oil in a frying pan and sauté the onion for about 6 minutes, stirring occasionally until softened. Stir in the fresh tomatoes and cook for 2 to 3 minutes until heated through and beginning to soften into the onions. Add the tuna, sunblush tomatoes, balsamic vinegar, basil and salt and pepper and heat for 1 minute before stirring into the pasta.

Little Gem Cups

Instead of making sandwiches, why not use the boat-shaped leaves of gem lettuce leaves to hold delicious fillings?

Makes 6 little gem cups

Chicken and Mango Little Gems
6 gem lettuce leaves
75 g (3 oz) cooked chicken breast, shredded
75 g (3 oz) chopped ripe mango
½ spring onion, finely sliced
1 tablespoon lemon juice and 1 teaspoon lemon zest
2 teaspoons honey
1½ tablespoons light olive oil

Separate the leaves and lay out on a plate. Mix together the shredded chicken, mango and spring onion in a bowl. Mix together the lemon juice, zest, honey and olive oil and toss with the chicken mixture. Place a spoonful of the mixture into each lettuce leaf and serve straight away.

Makes 4 little gem cups

Prawn and Watercress Little Gems
100 g (4 oz) small cooked prawns
2 tablespoons light mayonnaise
1 tablespoon tomato ketchup
a handful of watercress, trimmed and chopped
a little paprika
4 gem lettuce leaves

Mix the prawns together with the mayonnaise and ketchup and stir in the chopped watercress. Spoon some of the mixture into each lettuce leaf and sprinkle with paprika.

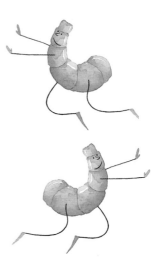

OTHER IDEAS FOR FILLINGS
- Ham, diced pineapple and cottage cheese
- Diced chicken, sweetcorn, light mayonnaise and spring onion
- Diced grilled chicken, salsa and low fat crème fraîche
- Diced chicken, light mayonnaise mixed with a little mild curry powder and a few raisins
- Shredded chicken, chopped tomato, chopped hard-boiled egg, alfalfa sprouts and mayonnaise
- Diced turkey, sunblush tomato, diced avocado and a little salad cream or mayonnaise
- Grated carrots, raisins and light mayonnaise
- Diced cherry tomatoes, mozzarella and basil with olive oil and balsamic vinegar
- Tinned tuna in brine mixed with low fat crème fraîche, a little tomato ketchup and sliced spring onions
- Tinned tuna mixed with chopped hard-boiled egg, sweetcorn, spring onion, salad cress and some light mayonnaise, mixed with a little white wine vinegar

Stir-fried Chicken with Broccoli

Stir-frying in a wok is a quick and easy method of cooking. Children tend to like Chinese food so making easy versions in your own kitchen can encourage children to enjoy eating vegetables. It is good to introduce new vegetables like shitake mushrooms, which have a lovely flavour.

Makes 4 portions

2 chicken breasts, cut into strips
salt
1 tablespoon sake (rice wine)
½ tablespoon cornflour
2½ tablespoons vegetable oil
1 clove garlic, crushed
1 onion, peeled and thinly sliced

1 medium carrot, peeled and cut into matchsticks
175 g (6 oz) broccoli, cut into small florets
75 g (3 oz) shitake mushrooms, finely sliced
100 ml (3 fl oz) chicken stock
1 tablespoon oyster sauce
½ teaspoon caster sugar
freshly ground black pepper

Season the strips of chicken with a little salt. Mix together the sake and cornflour, toss with the strips of chicken and set aside.

Heat 1 tablespoon of the oil in a wok, add half the garlic and the chicken and stir-fry for 2 minutes. Remove the chicken to a bowl and set aside.

Heat the remaining oil, add the garlic, onion and carrot and stir-fry for 3 minutes. Add the broccoli and mushrooms and stir-fry for 4 minutes.

Mix together the chicken stock, oyster sauce and sugar. Return the chicken to the wok, add the sauce and stir-fry for 1 minute. Season to taste.

Mini-Minute Steaks

This marinade is delicious and will also work well if you marinate cubes of fillet steak on a skewer and then cook them under a pre-heated grill, or on a griddle or barbecue.
Red meat is the best and most easily absorbed source of iron which is often lacking in children's diets.
By preparing meat yourself you can be sure to choose good lean cuts of beef.

Makes 2 portions

Marinade
1 tablespoon brown sugar
1 tablespoon soy sauce
½ tablespoon lime or lemon juice

2 x 125 g (4½ oz) minute steaks (very thin steaks)

1 tablespoon vegetable oil
1 clove garlic, crushed
1 medium carrot, peeled and cut into matchsticks
100 g (4 oz) courgette, cut into matchsticks
3 spring onions, thinly sliced
75 g (3 oz) beansprouts
75 ml (2½ fl oz) beef stock
½ teaspoon cornflour
1 tablespoon oyster sauce

Mix together the sugar, soy sauce and lime or lemon juice. Add the steaks and leave to marinate for at least 30 minutes.

Remove the steaks and reserve the marinade. Heat the vegetable oil in a wok and stir-fry the garlic for a few seconds. Add the carrot and stir-fry for 2 minutes. Add the courgettes, spring onion and beansprouts and stir-fry for 2 minutes. Mix a little of the beef stock with the cornflour to make a paste and then stir in the remaining beef stock and oyster sauce. Add this to the vegetables together with the reserved marinade, bring to the boil and cook for 1 minute until thickened slightly.

Brush a griddle pan with a few drops of vegetable oil. Pat the marinated steaks dry with some kitchen paper and cook the steaks on the griddle for just under 1 minute each side. Serve with the stir-fried vegetables and sauce.

Honey and Soy Salmon with Sesame

Not all fats are bad. The essential fatty acids in oily fish like salmon are good for boosting brain power – omega-3 essential fats optimise messaging between nerve cells in the brain. Good intakes are crucial for normal brain functioning and can be of particular benefit to dyslexic and hyperactive children.

Makes 2 portions

2 fillets salmon (approx. 150 g / 5 oz each)
2 tablespoons soy sauce
2 tablespoons runny honey
1 tablespoon rice wine vinegar
1 tablespoon vegetable oil

1 small onion, peeled and sliced
125 g (4½ oz) courgettes, cut into sticks 4 cm x ½ cm
75 g (3 oz) French beans, topped and tailed
1 heaped teaspoon toasted sesame seeds (dry-fry them over a medium heat, stirring until lightly golden)

Mix together the soy sauce, honey and rice wine vinegar. Place the salmon fillets in a dish and pour over the marinade. Leave to marinate for about 45 minutes. Pre-heat the grill to medium-high. Remove the fish from the marinade and place on a baking tray. Grill for about 5 minutes, brushing with the marinade halfway through. Meanwhile, heat the oil in a wok and stir-fry the onion for 2 minutes. Add the beans and stir-fry for 4 minutes. Add the courgette sticks and stir-fry for 3 minutes. Add the remaining marinade from the salmon and continue to stir-fry for about 30 seconds. Sprinkle half the toasted sesame seeds over the stir-fried vegetables. Sprinkle the remaining sesame seeds over the salmon and serve with the vegetables.

Marinated Griddled Chicken

Cooking on a griddle is an excellent way to cook without using very much fat. You can also cook salmon, tuna, steak or vegetables on the griddle. Always heat the griddle pan before you start cooking: this should take 2 to 3 minutes over a moderate to high heat. Once food has seared and a crust has formed, turn down the heat a little to ensure it cooks all the way through. Try this dish with thin slices of courgette, brushed with oil and griddled for a few minutes on each side.

Makes 2 portions

1½ tablespoons soy sauce
½ tablespoon light olive oil
1 tablespoon brown sugar

1 tablespoon freshly squeezed lemon juice
1 small clove garlic, peeled and chopped
2 chicken breasts

Mix together the soy sauce, olive oil, sugar, lemon juice and garlic in a bowl. Cover the chicken with cling film and bang with a mallet to flatten slightly. Add the chicken to the marinade and leave for 30 minutes to an hour. Remove the chicken from the marinade, strain and reserve. Heat the griddle, brush with a little vegetable oil and cook the chicken for about 3 minutes on each side or until cooked. Pour the strained marinade into a small saucepan, bring to the boil and simmer for 1 minute. Serve the chicken with the sauce.

Tropical Smoothie

Making smoothies for children is a great way to encourage them to consume valuable nutrients. Older children will enjoy blending the fruit themselves and making up their own combinations using fresh or frozen fruits, pure fruit juices and low fat yoghurt. *(See photograph, page 122.)*

Makes 2 glasses

½ large mango, peeled and stoned (approx. 200 g/ 7 oz mango flesh)
100 g (4 oz) fresh pineapple flesh or 1 small banana

250 ml (8 fl oz) freshly squeezed orange juice
2 passion fruits

Cut the mango and pineapple into cubes and blend together with the orange juice. Cut the passion fruits in half, scoop out the flesh and seeds and add to the orange juice mixture. Serve in glasses over ice.

Fruit Salad Smoothie

If you have time, freeze the banana already peeled in a plastic bag with the air pressed out.

Makes 2 glasses

100 g (4 oz) strawberries, hulled and cut into quarters
1 banana, peeled and sliced (can be frozen first)

1 large ripe peach, peeled, stoned and cut into pieces
150 ml (5 fl oz) low-fat strawberry drinking yoghurt
125 ml (4 fl oz) freshly squeezed orange juice

Simply whizz all the ingredients together in a blender.

Watermelon and Strawberry Refresher

This is good to make with blood oranges when they are in season.

Makes 2 glasses

400 g (1 lb) watermelon, flesh cut into cubes
150 g (5 oz) strawberries, hulled and cut in half

juice of 3 oranges
a little icing sugar, to sweeten

Simply blend together the watermelon, strawberries and orange juice and sweeten with sugar to taste.

Vegetarian Dishes

Perfect Chinese Fried Rice

This tends to be very popular with children and can be served as an accompaniment to many of the recipes in this book.

Makes 4 portions

200 g (7 oz) basmati rice
65 g (2½ oz) carrots, finely chopped
75 g (3 oz) frozen peas
5 ml (1 tsp) vegetable oil
1 egg, lightly beaten

25 g (1 oz) butter
65 g (2½ oz) onion, finely chopped
30 ml (2 tbsp) soy sauce
1 spring onion, finely sliced
salt and freshly ground black pepper

Cook the rice in a pan of lightly salted boiling water, together with the chopped carrots, according to the instructions on the packet. Four minutes before the end of the cooking time, add the frozen peas. Meanwhile, heat the vegetable oil in a frying pan or wok, beat the egg together with a little salt, tilt the pan so that the egg coats the base and cook until set as a thin omelette. Remove from the pan, roll up to form a sausage shape and cut into thin strips. Add the butter to the wok and sauté the onion for 2 minutes. Add the cooked rice mixture, the soy sauce and a little freshly ground black pepper. Stir-fry the rice for about 2 minutes. Stir in the strips of egg and spring onion and heat through.

Baked Marrow with a Cheesy Topping

If your child isn't too keen on eating vegetables, try this tasty recipe. It also makes a delicious accompaniment to an adult meal – it works especially well with poultry.

Makes 4 portions

1 medium-sized marrow
salt
1 onion, chopped
1 tablespoon parsley

30 ml (2 tbsp) vegetable oil
1 x 400 g (14 oz) can of chopped tomatoes
1 tablespoon fresh basil, torn into small pieces
100 g (4 oz) Cheddar cheese, grated

Peel and halve the marrow, scoop out the seeds and cut into 2.5 cm (1 in) cubes. Place in a colander, sprinkle with salt and leave for about 30 minutes. Rinse under the tap and pat dry.

Pre-heat the oven to 190°C/375°F/Gas 5. Sauté the onion and parsley in the oil until softened, add the tomatoes and cook for about 4 minutes. Add the marrow and basil, simmer for 10 to 15 minutes and season to taste. Transfer to an oven-proof dish, stir in 75 g (3 oz) of the cheese and sprinkle the remaining cheese on top. Bake in the oven for 30 minutes or until browned.

Cannelloni with Mushrooms and Ricotta

A good way to encourage children to eat more vegetables is to stuff them inside cannelloni. Try this tasty mushroom filling or mix some cooked spinach with ricotta, Parmesan and egg.

Makes 4–5 portions

2 tablespoons olive oil
1 onion, finely chopped
1 clove garlic, crushed
250 g (8½ oz) button mushrooms
250 g (8½ oz) chestnut (brown) mushrooms
250 g (8½ oz) ricotta cheese
60 g (2½ oz) grated Cheddar cheese
60 g (2½ oz) grated Parmesan
1 egg, lightly beaten
salt and pepper

Béchamel Sauce
30 g (1½ oz) butter
30 g (1½ oz) flour
375 ml (11 fl oz) milk
½ teaspoon nutmeg
salt and pepper

500 ml good quality bought tomato sauce
8 sheets lasagne or 10 cubes no pre-cook cannelloni

Pre-heat the oven to 180°C/350°F/Gas 4. Heat the oil over a medium heat and sauté the onion and garlic for 3 to 4 minutes. Add the mushrooms and sauté until the liquid has evaporated. Remove from the heat and stir in the ricotta, Cheddar, 40 g (1½ oz) of the Parmesan cheese, beaten egg and seasoning.

To make the béchamel sauce, melt the butter in a pan over a low heat. Stir in the flour and cook for 1 minute. Gradually whisk in the milk and nutmeg and season to taste.

If using fresh lasagne, cover the sheets of pasta in boiling water and leave for 5 minutes. Drain, then spoon some of the mushroom filling along the centre and fold in the two sides. Alternatively, using a teaspoon, spoon the mushroom filling into the no pre-cook cannelloni.

Spoon half the tomato sauce onto the bottom of a suitable ovenproof dish or make two smaller dishes and freeze one. Line up the filled tubes next to each other on top of the sauce. Cover with the remaining tomato sauce and then spread the béchamel sauce on top. Sprinkle with the remaining Parmesan cheese. Bake in the pre-heated oven for 25 to 30 minutes.

ANTIOXIDANTS

Vitamins A, C and E are known as antioxidants. They are thought to help protect against free radicals, destructive molecules that damage cells and DNA. If left unchecked, these unstable and potentially harmful chemicals can create conditions that may precipitate heart disease and cancer.

Summer Risotto

I like to make my risotto in a large frying pan. You will need to add the liquid to the rice little by little, waiting to add more until all the liquid has been absorbed and stirring frequently. It usually takes about 30 minutes to prepare, depending on your pan and your stove. Stir in a little extra stock if you need to re-heat the risotto.

Makes 4–6 portions

900 ml (1½ pints) vegetable stock or chicken stock
4 large shallots or one onion, finely chopped
1 garlic clove, crushed
40 g (1½ oz) butter
1 tablespoon olive oil
50 g (2 oz) red pepper, chopped

200 g (7 oz) arborio (risotto) rice
75 g (3 oz) courgette, diced
2 medium tomatoes, skinned, de-seeded and chopped (approx. 225 g/8 oz)
4 tablespoons white wine
40 g (1½ oz) Parmesan cheese, grated

Bring the stock to the boil and allow to simmer. Heat the oil and butter in a large frying pan and sauté the shallots and garlic for 1 minute. Add the red pepper and cooked for 5 minutes, stirring occasionally until softened. Add the rice and make sure that it is well coated. Stir for 1 minute. Add 1 or 2 ladlefuls of hot stock and simmer, stirring, until it has been absorbed, then add another ladleful of stock. Continue adding the stock a little at a time and simmer until the rice absorbs the liquid before adding more, stirring frequently. After 10 minutes, add the diced courgette and tomato. After about 8 minutes add the white wine. When all the stock has been added and the rice is cooked (it will probably take about 20 minutes for the rice to cook through), stir in the Parmesan cheese until melted and season to taste.

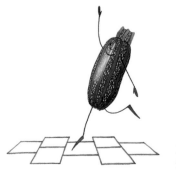

Perfect Baked Potatoes

The best potatoes to choose are floury varieties like Desirée, King Edward or Maris Piper. You can also make mini baked potatoes by using normal size potatoes, in which case the cooking time will be shorter. You could also try making baked sweet potatoes and serve these with butter and a little freshly ground black pepper.

Makes 4 portions

4 large baking potatoes
olive oil (optional)

salt and freshly ground black pepper
100 g (4 oz) cold butter

Pre-heat the oven to 200°C/400°F/Gas 6. Wash and dry the potatoes and prick the skins a few times with a fork. If you want extra crisp skins then rub the skins with a few drops of olive oil and sprinkle with a little salt before baking. Place on the centre shelf in the oven for 1 to 1½ hours (the cooking time will depend on the size of the potatoes). To check if the potatoes are cooked, squeeze gently to see if they feel soft. Alternatively, cook in the microwave (see below).

Cut a cross in the top of each potato and squeeze the sides to open them up. Sprinkle with a little salt and freshly ground black pepper and top with butter. Alternatively, cut each of the potatoes in half lengthways and scoop out the flesh and mash with a little milk, butter and seasoning.

TO MICROWAVE

Prick the potatoes as usual and wrap each one in absorbent kitchen paper. Cook on High for 6 to 7 minutes for one potato or about 12 minutes for two potatoes and 18 to 20 minutes for four potatoes (timings will differ depending on the size of the potatoes).

OTHER GOOD TOPPINGS

Sour cream and chives
Plain or curried baked beans
Tuna, mayonnaise and sweetcorn
Bacon cooked until crisp and then crumbled
Vegetables such as broccoli and carrots in a cheese sauce
Smoked ham, grated Cheddar cheese, crème fraîche or chives

Fluffy Baked Potatoes

Makes 4 portions

4 baking potatoes, scrubbed and pricked
50 g (2 oz) butter
45 ml (3 tbsp) double cream or milk

2 eggs, separate
75 g (3 oz) Cheddar cheese, grated
salt and freshly ground black pepper

Pre-heat the oven to 190°C/375°F/Gas 5. Cut each potato in half, scoop out the flesh into a large saucepan leaving enough around the sides so that they still retain their shape. Add the butter, cream, egg yolks and 50 g (2 oz) of the cheese to the potato flesh. Mash together until smooth and season to taste. Whisk the egg whites until stiff and fold into the potato mixture. Carefully spoon this back into the potato skins and sprinkle with the remaining grated cheese. Bake in the oven for 15 minutes until golden. Serve immediately.

Mini Baked Potatoes

For a change, how about making mini baked potatoes using new potatoes. The potato's best source of fibre and nutrients is in the skin and in the flesh just under the skin. Potatoes are a good source of carbohydrate, which provides energy, and are also a useful and cheap source of vitamin C.

Makes 4 portions

450 g (1 lb) new potatoes
15 ml (1 tbsp) olive oil
1 teaspoon dried mixed herbs
2 teaspoons coarse sea salt

Toppings
Sour cream and chives
Hummus
Taramasalata
Tuna mayonnaise and sweetcorn
Baked beans
Cottage cheese with chives

Pre-heat the oven to 200°C/400°F/Gas 6. Scrub and dry the potatoes. Prick the skins with a fork and mix them with the olive oil and herbs, tossing them in a bowl to coat. Place the potatoes on a baking sheet and sprinkle with the sea salt. Bake for 25 to 30 minutes or until they are crisp and tender. Cut a cross in the top of each potato, squeeze them gently to open them up and fill with a topping of your choice or just simply with a knob of butter.

Gratin of Courgette

This has a light soufflé-type consistency and makes a delicious light lunch with a salad or can be served as a tasty accompaniment to a meal and looks elegant enough for a dinner party. (*See photograph opposite*)

Makes 6 portions

45 ml (3 tbsp) vegetable oil
500 g (1 lb 2 oz) courgettes, topped and tailed
and thinly sliced
salt and freshly ground black pepper

2 tablespoons chopped fresh parsley
4 eggs
125 ml (4 fl oz) crème fraîche
150 g (5 oz) Gruyère cheese, grated

Pre-heat the oven to 180°C/350°F/Gas 4. Heat the oil in a frying pan and season the courgettes with some salt and freshly ground black pepper. Sauté these together with the parsley over a low heat for about 20 minutes or until softened. Using a fork, beat the eggs, then beat in the crème fraîche, Gruyère cheese and a little seasoning. Stir in the courgettes and spoon the mixture into an oven-proof dish measuring approximately 25 x 20 cm (10 x 8 in) and cook in the oven for 20 to 25 minutes.

Courgette Fritters

If your children aren't keen on eating vegetables then try these – they are delicious and were very popular with my tasting panel – even the confirmed vegetable haters.

Makes 4 portions

450 g (1 lb) courgettes
salt and freshly ground black pepper
250 ml (8 fl oz) water

4 tablespoons cornflour
8 tablespoons plain flour
vegetable oil for deep frying

Wash and dry the courgettes and trim off the ends. Cut them into sticks about 6 cm (2¼ in) long and 2 cm (¾ in) wide and season them with salt and pepper. Beat together the water, cornflour, plain flour and some salt and pepper to form a thin batter.

Heat the oil in a deep fat fryer with a basket filled with oil to a depth of about 5 cm (2 in). Alternatively, you could use a heavy pan and a metal slotted spoon or strainer. Heat the oil until it reaches a temperature of 190°C/375°F (you can tell when it is hot enough for frying if a piece of vegetable sizzles as it touches the oil). Dip the courgette sticks into the batter and fry them until crispy and golden. Lift out the basket or remove the courgette fritters with a slotted spoon or strainer. Drain on absorbent paper and serve immediately.

Super Vegetarian Spring Rolls

Spring rolls are actually quite easy to make and children love them. These are filled with vegetables and rice noodles and are bound to be a great hit! Spring rolls can be frozen and reheated in a hot oven.

Makes 24 spring rolls

2 tablespoons vegetable oil
1 medium onion, sliced
1 clove garlic, crushed
75 g (3 oz) carrots, cut into thin strips
75 g (3 oz) red pepper, cut into thin strips
350 g (12 oz) white cabbage, shredded
150 g (6 oz) beansprouts
250 g (8 oz) button mushrooms, cut into thin strips
2 spring onions, finely sliced
75 g (3 oz) fine rice noodles
1 tablespoon cornflour
1 tablespoon water
1 tablespoon oyster sauce
½ tablespoon soy sauce

1 teaspoon sugar
1 vegetable stock cube
24 spring roll wrappers
1 egg, beaten
vegetable oil for deep frying

Dipping sauce
4 tablespoons rice wine vinegar
1 tablespoon soft brown sugar
4 tablespoons sake (Japanese rice wine)
1 tablespoon soy sauce
½ red chilli, de-seeded and finely sliced
1 tablespoon finely sliced spring onion (optional)

Heat the oil in a wok or frying pan and stir-fry the onion and garlic until lightly golden. Add the carrot and red pepper and stir-fry for 3 minutes. Add the cabbage, beansprouts, mushrooms and spring onions and stir-fry for 3 to 4 minutes. Cook the rice noodles according to the instructions on the packet and then rinse in a colander under cold water. Cut the noodles into short lengths of about 2.5 cm (1 inch). Stir the cornflour into the water and combine with the oyster sauce, soy sauce and sugar. Add the noodles to the vegetables in the wok, pour in the sauce and crumble over the stock cube. Stir-fry, mixing everything together for 2 minutes.

Fold over one corner of each spring roll wrapper. Place 2 to 3 tablespoons of the filling about one third of the way down. Roll over once, fold in both ends and roll over to form a spring roll. Brush the remaining corner with some beaten egg and press down to seal. To cook the spring rolls, heat the oil in a wok or deep fryer until hot, then reduce the heat. Deep-fry the spring rolls in batches for 2 to 3 minutes or until lightly golden and crispy, then remove and drain on kitchen paper.

To make the sauce, place the vinegar and sugar in a pan and dissolve over a gentle heat. Bring to the boil and then simmer for 3 minutes until slightly reduced. Add the rice wine and bring to the boil, then remove from the heat and stir in the soy sauce. Allow to cool down a little and then stir in the chilli and spring onion (if using).

Cheesy Vegetable Sausages

If you are finding it difficult to get your child to enjoy eating vegetables, try these delicious vegetarian sausages which are quick and easy to prepare. If you have time you can form the mixture into sausage shapes and then set aside in the freezer to firm up before frying. As a variation, add a teaspoon of green pesto, which interestingly tends to be quite popular with children. *(See photograph, page 132.)*

Makes 8 sausages

225 g (8 oz) sliced white bread
50 g (2 oz) grated carrot
175 g (6 oz) grated courgette
25 g (1 oz) butter
1 medium onion, finely chopped

150 g (5 oz) grated Cheddar cheese
1 egg, separated
a little salt and pepper
oil, for frying

Make the breadcrumbs by tearing the bread into pieces and blitzing it in a food processor. Squeeze the excess liquid out of the carrot and courgette.

Heat the butter in a frying pan and fry the onion until soft. Add the grated carrot and cook for 2 minutes. Add the courgette and cook for 3 minutes until softened. Mix with the grated cheese, half the breadcrumbs, the egg yolk and seasoning.

Shape into 8 sausages about 10 cm/4 inches long, using floured hands and chill in the freezer for 10 minutes. Dip into the lightly beaten egg white and then roll in the remaining breadcrumbs. Heat some oil in a wok or frying pan and shallow-fry the sausages until lightly golden.

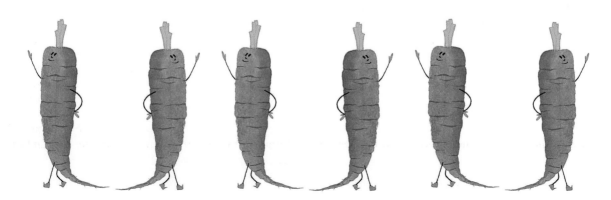

Caramelised Onion and Gruyère Tart

This is my favourite recipe for quiche and the slow cooking of the onions gives them a delicious flavour. The pastry takes only a few minutes to make in a food processor, but you could use bought shortcrust pastry instead.

Makes 8 portions

Pastry
225 g (8 oz) plain flour
a pinch of salt
½ teaspoon mustard powder
125 g (4½ oz) butter, diced
45 ml (3 tbsp) cold water

Filling
500 g (1 lb 2 oz) onions, thinly sliced
15 ml (1 tbsp) vegetable oil
15 g (½ oz) butter
salt and freshly ground black pepper
4 eggs
300 ml (½ pint) milk
300 ml (½ pint) single cream
150 g (5 oz) Gruyère cheese, grated
25 g (1 oz) Parmesan cheese, grated

Put the flour, salt, mustard powder and butter in a food processor and process until the mixture resembles soft breadcrumbs. Gradually add enough water to form a good consistency. Press into a ball with your hands and chill in the fridge for at least 30 minutes.

Pre-heat the oven to 220°C/425°F/Gas 7. To make the filling, heat the vegetable oil and the butter in a large frying pan and sauté the onions over a fairly high heat for about 5 minutes. Lower the heat and cook for a further 20 minutes, cover with non-stick baking paper, and stir occasionally until the onions are caramelised. Season with a little salt. Lightly beat the eggs, stir in the milk, cream and the grated Gruyère cheese. Season with a little pepper and stir in the caramelised onions.

Grease a 25 x 4 cm (10 x 1½ in) deep loose-bottomed flan tin. On a lightly floured work surface, roll out the dough and line the base and sides of the flan tin. Prick the base of the pastry and bake blind in an oven for 10 minutes. Remove the baking paper and the beans, turn down the temperature to 190°C/375°F/Gas 5 and cook for a further 5 minutes. Spoon the onion mixture into the flan case and sprinkle with the Parmesan cheese. Bake in the oven for 20 to 25 minutes.

The Caramelised Onion and Gruyère Tart is shown overleaf

Vegetable Burgers

These vegetable burgers are delicious eaten either hot or cold.

Makes 8 vegetable burgers

2 medium carrots, grated
1 medium courgette, grated
1 onion, chopped
50 g (2 oz) chestnut or button mushrooms, chopped
75 g (3 oz) cashew nuts, roughly chopped
1 tablespoon chopped fresh oregano or ½ teaspoon dried oregano
1 tablespoon chopped fresh parsley

a pinch of cayenne pepper (optional)
150 g (5 oz) fresh brown breadcrumbs plus 100 g (4 oz) for coating
15 ml (1 tbsp) tomato sauce
7.5 ml (½ tbsp) soy sauce
½ small egg
salt and freshly ground black pepper
vegetable oil for frying

Using your hands, squeeze out some of the excess moisture from the grated carrots and courgette. In a large bowl, mix together the vegetables, cashew nuts, herbs, cayenne pepper and 150 g (5 oz) of the breadcrumbs. Beat together the tomato sauce, soy sauce and the half egg, stir this into the vegetable mixture and season. Using your hands, form the mixture into eight burgers and coat with the remaining breadcrumbs. At this stage you can set the burgers aside in the fridge to firm up, but it is not essential. Sauté the burgers in vegetable oil, turning occasionally until they are golden.

Mashed Potato with Carrot

There are lots of different ways to turn ordinary mashed potatoes into something special. This is one of my favourites. For a really smooth texture you can add a little more butter and milk. Mashed potato and sweet potato with milk, butter and a little grated Parmesan cheese is also delicious.

Makes 3 portions

450 g (1 lb) potatoes, peeled and chopped
1 large carrot, thinly sliced
25 g (1 oz) butter

15 ml (1 tbsp) milk
salt and freshly ground black pepper

Put the potatoes and carrot into a pan of lightly salted water. Bring to the boil and then cook for about 20 minutes or until the vegetables are tender. Drain and then mash together with the butter, milk and seasoning until quite smooth. You can make lovely domes of mash using an ice cream scoop.

Ratatouille Omelette

This concoction of sautéed Mediterranean vegetables mixed with eggs and topped with grated cheese in the style of a Spanish omelette is quite delicious and a meal in itself. (*See photograph, opposite.*)

Serves 6

1 aubergine, sliced
1 small onion, sliced
45 ml (3 tbsp) olive oil
1 large courgette, sliced
1 red pepper, cored, de-seeded and cut into
strips
2 tomatoes, skinned, de-seeded and chopped

salt and freshly ground black pepper
6 eggs
30 ml (2 tbsp) cold water
25 g (1 oz) butter
75 ml (3 fl oz) double cream
75 g (3 oz) Gruyère cheese, grated

Gently sauté the onion in olive oil in a heavy-based frying pan until soft. Chop the aubergine and add with the courgette and pepper, cover the pan and cook for about 20 minutes or until the vegetables are soft but not mushy. Add the tomatoes and cook for a further 5 minutes. Season to taste. Lightly whisk the eggs with the cold water, then mix in the cooked vegetables. Heat the butter in a deep 25-cm (10-in) omelette or frying pan. When the butter is frothy, pour the egg mixture into the pan and cook until set. Remove from the heat, pour over the double cream and cover with the grated cheese. Cook under a pre-heated grill for a few minutes until golden. Leave the handle of the frying pan sticking out of the grill and cover with aluminium foil if necessary.

Delicious Vegetable Rissoles

I make fresh breadcrumbs for this recipe by putting 2 slices of wholemeal bread in a food processor.

Makes 12 rissoles

75 g (3 oz) white of leek, finely chopped
150 g (5 oz) carrots, grated
100 g (4 oz) butternut squash, grated
100 g (4 oz) button mushrooms, finely chopped
1 tablespoon freshly chopped parsley

100 g (4 oz) wholemeal breadcrumbs
10 ml (2 tsp) soy sauce
1 egg, lightly beaten
salt and freshly ground black pepper
vegetable oil for frying

Sauté the leek for 2 minutes and squeeze some of the juices from the grated carrots and squash. Mix together wih the remaining vegetables, parsley, breadcrumbs, soy sauce, beaten egg and seasoning and chop for a few seconds in a food processor. Using your hands, form into about 12 rissoles. Heat the oil in a large frying pan and sauté the rissoles over a medium heat for 8 to 10 minutes, turning occasionally until golden and cooked through.

Spotted Snake Pizza

This pizza is great fun to make together with your child. It almost looks too good to eat!

15 g (½ oz) active dried yeast
250 ml (8 fl oz) lukewarm water
a pinch of sugar
30 ml (2 tbsp) olive oil
400 g (14 oz) strong white flour
1 teaspoon salt
75 g (3 oz) Cheddar cheese
1 egg, lightly beaten

Topping
10 tablespoons ready-made tomato sauce with herbs
200 g (7 oz) Mozzarella cheese, cut into slices
red, orange and yellow mini peppers, cored and de-seeded
2 black olives, stoned
small piece of green pepper

Place the yeast in a mixing bowl, pour over the warm water, stir in the sugar and mix with a fork. Allow to stand until the yeast has dissolved and starts to foam (about 10 minutes). Stir in the olive oil, mix the flour and salt together and fold half of this mixture into the bowl using a wooden spoon. Gradually mix in three-quarters of the remaining flour, stirring with the spoon until the dough forms a sticky mass and begins to come away from the sides of the bowl.

Sprinkle some of the remaining flour on to a smooth work surface. Remove the dough from the bowl and gradually knead in the remaining flour, a little at a time, until the dough is smooth and elastic and no longer sticks to your hands. This will probably take between 8 and 10 minutes. Form into a ball and place in an oiled bowl, cover with a damp tea-towel and leave in a warm place to rise for about 50 minutes, or until doubled in size. To test whether the dough has risen enough, stick two fingers in the dough and if the indentations remain, the dough is ready. Punch the dough down with your fist and place on a floured work surface. Knead again for a few minutes until the dough is nice and elastic.

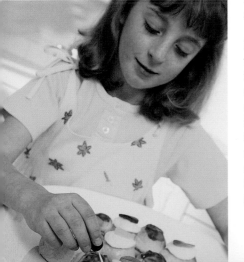

Pre-heat the oven to 200°C/400°F/Gas 6. Divide the dough into about 12 balls with one larger ball for the head of the snake and make a small tail from the dough for the end of the snake. Stuff each of the balls with a small cube of Cheddar cheese, making sure it is completely covered with dough. Place the balls and tail on a large greased baking tray in the shape of a snake so that they are just touching each other. Brush the tops of the balls with beaten egg and cook in the oven for 10 minutes, or until lightly golden and joined together. Top each ball alternately with tomato sauce and a slice of Mozzarella cheese, and decorate with mini sweet pepper shapes, which can be cut out using mini biscuit cutters. Bake for a further 5 minutes. Add olives for eyes and a forked tongue cut out from a strip of green pepper to complete the snake.

Cakes and Biscuits

Apple, Honey and Raisin Muffins

Honey and apple combine to make a light, moist muffin, and the apple disappears in the mixture so fussier children won't notice it. If you don't have a food processor, grate the apple finely, beat it together with the wet ingredients, and then fold it into the dry ingredients. I've added chopped dried apple on top to give a bit more interest, but a quarter or half ring of dried apple on the top of each would also look attractive.

Makes 8

85 g (3½ oz) self-raising flour
½ teaspoon ground cinnamon
½ teaspoon ground ginger
¼ teaspoon salt
50 g (2 oz) butter, at room temperature
50 g (2 oz) soft light brown sugar

85 g (3½ oz) clear honey
1 egg
½ teaspoon vanilla extract
½ large apple, peeled, cored and grated
50 g (2 oz) raisins
25 g (1 oz) chopped dried apple (optional)

Pre-heat the oven to 180°C/350°F/Gas 4. Line a muffin tin with 8 paper cases.

Sift the flour, cinnamon, ginger and salt into a bowl and set aside. Put the butter, sugar, honey, egg, vanilla and apple in a food processor and whiz for about 1 minute until well combined (the mixture will look a little curdled but don't worry).

Add the flour mixture and pulse twice, then scrape down the sides of the food processor and pulse 2–3 times. Add the raisins and pulse for a further 2 times, just to mix in the raisins without chopping them.

Spoon the batter into the paper cases; they should be about half full. Scatter the dried apple over the tops. Bake for 20–22 minutes, until well risen and firm to the touch. Cool for about 10 minutes in the tin, then transfer to a wire rack to cool. Store in an airtight container.

Funny Face Fairy Cakes

These are always very popular at children's birthday parties, decorated with faces made from a mixture of small sweets and writing icing. My children adore making their own funny faces. You can also make miniature fairy cakes for young children using paper cases for confectionery and baking the cakes in a mini-muffin tin.

Makes 10 cupcakes

100 g (4 oz) self-raising flour
100 g (4 oz) soft margarine
100 g (4 oz) caster sugar
2 eggs
5 ml (1 tsp) vanilla essence
½ teaspoon grated lemon rind (optional)
75 g (3 oz) raisins or sultanas (optional)

Icing
175 g (6 oz) icing sugar, sifted
water
small tubes of coloured writing icing
Liquorice Allsorts, Dolly Mixtures, Smarties, Jelly Tots

Pre-heat the oven to 180°C/350°F/Gas 4. Put the larger paper cases in a bun tray and the sweet cases in a mini-muffin tray. Sieve the self-raising flour into a mixing bowl. Add the margarine, caster sugar and eggs and beat everything together until the mixture is soft and creamy. Beat in the vanilla essence and grated lemon rind, if using. If you don't want to decorate the fairy cakes, you could make plump raisin or sultana cupcakes by folding raisins or sultanas into the batter at this stage.

Spoon the batter into the cases until about two-thirds full. Bake the larger cakes in the oven for about 20 minutes, and the smaller cakes for about 12 minutes or until a cocktail stick inserted into the centre comes out clean. Turn them on to a wire rack to cool.

To make the icing, sift the icing sugar into a bowl and gradually stir in a little water to make a thick smooth paste. Once the cakes are cool, ice and decorate them.

Raspberry Ripple Cheesecake

The combination of cream cheese and fresh raspberry purée makes this the most fabulous cheesecake. It is surprisingly easy to make and requires no baking. It's important, though, to use the cream cheese at room temperature, otherwise the gelatine will harden too quickly and go lumpy.

Makes 8 portions

7 gelatine leaves (approx. 12 g) or 1 x 11 g sachet powdered gelatine
200 g (7 oz) digestive biscuits
100 g (4 oz) butter
150 g (5 oz) fresh raspberries
2 tablespoons icing sugar
1 tablespoon cornflour

450 g (1 lb) cream cheese, at room temperature
225 g (8 oz) caster sugar
2 teaspoons vanilla extract
400 ml (12 fl oz) double cream
300 g (10 oz) fresh berries for topping, e.g. raspberries, strawberries, blackberries
85 g (3½ oz) white chocolate

If using gelatine leaves, soak them in 150 ml (5 fl oz) water for 5 minutes, then remove, squeezing out any excess water, and place in a bowl set over a pan of simmering water for about 30 seconds, stirring until melted. Set aside to cool. If using powdered gelatine, put 3 tablespoons water into a small saucepan, sprinkle over the gelatine and leave to stand for 5 minutes. Put the pan over a very low heat and stir gently for 1 minute until the gelatine has dissolved. Set aside to cool.

Break the biscuits into pieces, place in a plastic bag and crush with a rolling pin. Melt the butter in a large pan and stir in the biscuits. Spread the mixture over the base of a 20 cm (8 inch) cake tin, pressing it down, then place in the fridge.

Blitz the raspberries together with the icing sugar in a food processor, then press through a sieve into a small pan to get rid of the seeds. Remove 1 tablespoon of the raspberry coulis and mix with the cornflour. Stir this into the raspberry coulis in the pan, bring to the boil, then remove from the heat and allow to cool. It should thicken up nicely.

Beat together the cream cheese, sugar and vanilla until smooth. Remove about 6 tablespoons and stir into the gelatine. Beat the cream until stiff. Fold the cream into the cream cheese mixture, together with the cream cheese and gelatine mixture.

Remove the cake tin from the fridge and spread half the cheesecake mixture over the base. Spoon half the raspberry coulis in blobs onto the cheesecake mix and then, using a skewer, swirl it through to make a ripple effect. Spoon the remaining cheesecake mixture on top and carefully spread out so as not to disturb the layer underneath. Level the surface with a palette knife. Decorate the top of the cake by trailing lines of raspberry coulis dropped from a teaspoon held horizontally across the cake. Using a skewer, draw vertical lines through the coulis to create a pattern. Set aside in the fridge to set.

The cake can be served as it is. Alternatively, arrange the berries on top. Melt the chocolate in a heatproof bowl over a pan of simmering water. Fill a piping bag with a small plain writing nozzle and pipe zig-zag lines of chocolate over the fruit.

Annabel's Apricot Cookies

This fabulous and rather unusual combination of dried apricots and white chocolate makes irresistible cookies. Once you have sampled these you will probably want to double the quantities second time around.

Makes 26 cookies

100 g (4 oz) unsalted butter
100 g (4 oz) cream cheese
100 g (4 oz) caster sugar
75 g (3 oz) plain flour

50 g (2 oz) chopped dried apricots
65 g (2½ oz) white chocolate chips or chopped white chocolate

Pre-heat the oven to 180°C/350°F/Gas 4. In a large mixing bowl, cream together the butter and cream cheese. Add the sugar and beat until fluffy. Gradually add the flour, then fold in the apricots and chocolate. The dough will be quite soft – don't worry! Drop the mixture by heaped teaspoons on to baking sheets lined with non-stick baking paper and bake in the oven for 15 minutes or until lightly golden. Allow to cool and harden for a few minutes before removing them from the baking sheet.

Teddy Bear Fairy Cakes

Children love decorating these tasty lemon-flavoured fairy cakes with teddy bear faces and they are very popular for birthday parties. Or how about making a teddy bear's picnic with sandwiches and biscuits cut into the shape of teddy bears? Instead of both lemon and lime zest, you could use just lemon zest. *(See photograph, opposite.)*

Makes 6 fairy cakes

2 eggs
100 g (4 oz) butter, softened
100 g (4 oz) self-raising flour
1 teaspoon baking powder
1 tablespoon Greek yoghurt
100 g (4 oz) golden caster sugar
zest of ½ lemon, finely grated
zest of ½ lime, finely grated

6 teaspoons lemon curd

Decoration
Smarties or M&Ms for eyes
chocolate buttons for ears
Jelly Tots for noses
tubes of writing icing (available in small tubes in most supermarkets)

Pre-heat the oven to 180°C/350°F/Gas 4. Line a muffin tin with 6 paper cases. Measure all the cake ingredients except for the lemon curd into the bowl of an electric mixer and whisk together until just combined. Using a spoon, half fill the 6 paper cases. Spoon a teaspoonful of lemon curd on top of each, then spoon the remaining cake mixture on top. Bake in the oven for 15–20 minutes, until lightly golden and well risen. Leave to cool on a wire rack. When cool, attach the Smarties eyes, Jelly Tot noses and chocolate button ears using writing icing. Also use the writing icing to add pupils to the eyes and to draw on mouths.

Cranberry and White Chocolate Cookies

These are not to be missed: probably my favourite cookies and so quick and easy to make. You can buy dried cranberries in the supermarket. *(See photograph, opposite.)*

Makes 20 cookies

150 g (5 oz) plain flour
½ teaspoon bicarbonate of soda
½ teaspoon salt
25 g (1 oz) ground almonds
150 g (5 oz) soft brown sugar

50 g (2 oz) porridge oats
50 g (2 oz) dried cranberries
40 g (1½ oz) white chocolate, cut into chunks
150 g (5 oz) butter
1 large egg yolk or 2 small egg yolks

Pre-heat the oven to 190°C/375°F/Gas 5. Sieve together the flour, bicarbonate of soda and salt in a large bowl. Stir in the ground almonds, brown sugar, porridge oats, cranberries and white chocolate chunks.

Melt the butter in a small pan. Stir this into the dry ingredients together with the egg yolk. Mix well, then using your hands form into walnut-sized balls and arrange on two large non-stick baking sheets. Gently press them down to flatten slightly, leaving space between them for the biscuits to spread. Bake in the oven for 12 minutes, then remove and allow to cool on a wire rack.

M&M Cookies

Children will love helping you make these cookies, which are studded with brightly coloured candy-coated chocolate. If you find the candy cracks open when baked you can remove the cookies from the oven, and add the extra M&Ms on top halfway through baking so that they are only baked in the oven for 5 minutes. *(See photograph, page 152.)*

Makes 20 cookies

75 g (3 oz) brown sugar
75 g (3 oz) granulated sugar
25 g (1 oz) butter
15 g (½ oz) white vegetable shortening
1 teaspoon pure vanilla essence

1 egg
175 g (6 oz) plain flour
½ teaspoon baking soda
½ teaspoon salt
150 g (5 oz) candy-coated chocolate M&Ms

Pre-heat the oven to 180°C/350°F/Gas 4. Mix together the sugars, butter, shortening, vanilla and egg. Sift together the flour, baking powder and salt and stir into the butter and sugar mixture. Mix in 100 g (4 oz) of the M&Ms. Using your hands, shape the dough into walnut-sized balls and spread well apart on ungreased baking sheets. Flatten slightly and press the remaining M&Ms into the dough to decorate the cookies. Bake for about 10 minutes until lightly golden. The centres will be soft but will firm up later. Allow to cool a little before removing from the baking sheets and placing on a wire rack.

Annabel's No-bake Train Cake

The beauty of this cake is that it requires no cooking and can be created in very little time from basic ready-made ingredients. Older children will enjoy helping you assemble it but watch out that they don't eat the ingredients first as it's made out of all the things that children love. You can choose any selection of sweets for the goods carriages.

Serves 20

Grass
2 x 250 g (8½ oz) packets desiccated coconut
1 x 38 ml (1½ oz) edible green food colouring
water
75 ml (5 tbsp) apricot jam

Chocolate buttercream
75 g (3 oz) butter, softened
125 g (4½ oz) icing sugar
1 tablespoon cocoa powder
15 ml (1 tbsp) milk

5 x 205 g (7 oz) large chocolate-covered swiss
roll filled with chocolate buttercream
1 milk chocolate marshmallow tea cake

1 chocolate Rolo
1 x 227 g (8 oz) packet Liquorice Allsorts
1 packet of liquorice catherine wheels
1 box chocolate sticks
1 x 150 g (5 oz) box white chocolate fingers
1 x 150 g (5 oz) box milk chocolate fingers
20 milk chocolate-coated mini swiss rolls
6 raspberry jam sandwich creams

1 x 150 g (5 oz) packet of fizzy strawberry
and cream flavour lances
1 x 100 g (4 oz) packet Dolly Mixtures
1 x 200 g (7 oz) packet mini marshmallows
2 mini packets assorted sweets

To make the grass to cover the cake board, thoroughly mix the desiccated coconut with a little of the green food colouring and a few drops of water. Warm the apricot jam and brush it over the surface of two 40 x 30 cm (16 x 12 in) silver cake boards. The cake boards can be stuck together first if you like or if you are going to transport the cake, it's probably best if they are left separate. Strew the green coconut over the cake boards and press down on to the board so that they are completely covered.

To make the chocolate buttercream, beat the softened butter until creamy. Sift the icing sugar and cocoa powder into the bowl and beat together with the butter. Finally, beat in the milk. Cut about 5 cm (2 in) off the end of one of the large chocolate swiss rolls and secure this on top of a whole large chocolate Swiss roll to form the engine with some of the chocolate buttercream or a cocktail stick to form the cab. Secure a chocolate marshmallow tea cake with a Rolo to form the chimney. Attach two Liquorice Allsorts to form the windows of the cab. Attach a liquorice catherine wheel to the front of the cab with some of the buttercream. If you like, attach cotton wool balls on to a length of wire to look like steam coming from the engine.

Annabel's No-bake Train Cake is shown overleaf

Lay out the track using two parallel lines of chocolate sticks in a zigzag pattern and lay white chocolate and milk chocolate fingers alternately across the track to form the railway line. You will need to allow for the engine and five carriages. Put five mini milk chocolate rolls at the front of the track to form the bumper and the wheels of the engine and balance the engine on top. Attach three raspberry sandwich cream biscuits to each side of the engine with some of the buttercream to form the wheels and decorate the front with three Liquorice Allsorts. Cut a thin slice off the top of the remaining large chocolate Swiss rolls to form the carriages of the train and spread the flat surfaces with some of the chocolate buttercream. Lay each of the carriages over the mini swiss rolls along the track. Pile the sweets on to the open trucks.

Coconut Kisses

I defy you to eat only one of these! They're definitely one of my favourites, and your children will enjoy helping you make as well as eat them.

Makes 25 biscuits

100 g (4 oz) butter
50 g (2 oz) soft brown sugar
50 g (2 oz) caster sugar
1 egg, beaten
2.5 ml (½ tsp) pure vanilla extract
75 g (3 oz) plain flour

½ teaspoon baking soda
½ teaspoon salt
120 g (4½ oz) plain chocolate chips
75 g (3 oz) rolled oats
40 g (1½ oz) desiccated coconut

Pre-heat the oven to 180°C/350°F/Gas 4. Cream together the butter and sugars. Add the egg and vanilla. Sift together the flour, baking soda and salt and beat this into the mixture. Stir in the chocolate chips, oats and coconut. Form into walnut-sized balls, flatten the top with your hand and place spaced apart on a lightly greased or lined baking tray. Bake in the oven for 10–15 minutes. The biscuits will harden when they cool down.

Strawberry Cream Cake

A simple and quick cake to make – and it's sure to be a great favourite with everyone in the family.

Makes 8 portions

175 g (6 oz) soft margarine
175 g (6 oz) soft brown sugar
3 large eggs, beaten
175 g (6 oz) self-raising flour
½ teaspoon lemon zest
5 ml (1 tsp) vanilla essence
15 ml (1 tbsp) water

Filling/topping

300 ml (½ pint) whipping or double cream
3 tablespoons icing sugar
150 g (6 oz) strawberries
30-45 ml (2-3 tbsp) strawberry jam

Pre-heat the oven to 180°C/350°F/Gas 4 and line and grease two 20 cm (8 in) sandwich tins. Beat together the margarine and sugar, then add the eggs, one at a time, adding 1 tablespoon of flour with the eggs after the first egg to stop the mixture from curdling. Beat in the remaining flour, the lemon zest, vanilla essence and water until light and fluffy.

Divide the mixture between the prepared sandwich tins and bake in the oven for about 20 minutes or until lightly golden and risen. Turn them out of the tins and put on a wire rack to cool.

Whip the cream with the icing sugar until firm. Thinly slice 100 g (4 oz) of the strawberries. Stir the strawberries into two-thirds of the whipped cream. Spread the strawberry jam over one of the cakes, top with the strawberries and cream mixture and place the other cake on top. Using the remaining cream, pipe rosettes around the cake and place half a strawberry on top of each rosette. Keep refrigerated until ready to serve.

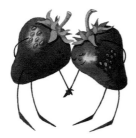

Apple Smiles

This snack is easy to prepare and will certainly bring a smile to your child's face! For a healthier variation, use small cubes of cheese instead of mini marshmallows. *(See photograph, opposite.)*

Makes 4 apple smiles

1 red apple, cored and sliced into eighths
a squeeze of lemon juice

smooth peanut butter
miniature marshmallows

Spread peanut butter on one side of each apple slice (squeeze a little lemon juice over the apple if not serving immediately). Place four miniature marshmallows on one apple slice and then lay another apple slice peanut butter side down on top.

Divinely Decadent Fruity Dark Chocolate Bars

These no-bake chocolate fruit and nut bars are amazingly good and one of my favourite treats. Indulge yourself and make sure they're hidden when Daddy or Mummy comes home. They are also fun for children to make themselves.

Makes 12 bars

200 g (7 oz) good-quality plain chocolate
75 g (3 oz) unsalted butter
1 x 397 g (14 oz) can of condensed milk
225 g (8 oz) digestive biscuits, broken into pieces

100 g (4 oz) ready-to-eat dried apricots, roughly chopped
50 g (2 oz) raisins
60 g (2½ oz) pecans, roughly chopped

Break the chocolate into squares and cut the butter into pieces, put these into a suitable dish together with the butter, and microwave on full power for about 3 minutes, stirring halfway through. (Alternatively, the chocolate and butter can be melted in a bowl over a saucepan of simmering water.) Stir the condensed milk into the chocolate mixture and mix in the broken biscuits, chopped apricots, raisins and chopped pecans. Line an 18 x 28 cm (7 x 11 in) shallow cake tin with clear film, allowing the sides to overhang. Spoon the mixture into the tin and press down but still leaving the top a little rough. Place in the fridge to set. Once set, lift the cake out of the tin by the overhanging clear film and cut into small bars. Keep chilled in the fridge.

Glossy Dark and White Chocolate Brownies

Two chocolates are combined to make these irresistible squares of rich, chewy brownies. (*See photograph, opposite.*)

**Makes 16
squares**

150 g (5 oz) dark chocolate, chopped
75 g (3 oz) unsalted butter
5 ml (1 tsp) pure vanilla extract
100 g (4 oz) caster sugar
2 eggs
1 egg yolk
90 g (3½ oz) plain flour
¼ teaspoon salt

150 g (5 oz) white chocolate buttons or
chipped white chocolate

Chocolate satin glaze
75 g (3 oz) dark chocolate, chopped
15 g (½ oz) unsalted butter
50 g (2 oz) white chocolate buttons

Pre-heat the oven to 180°C/350°F/Gas 4 and line and grease a 20 cm (8 in) square baking pan. Melt the dark chocolate and butter in a microwave for 2 minutes on High (or in a saucepan over a gentle heat, stirring constantly). Stir in the vanilla and sugar, then add the eggs and yolk, one at a time, stirring after each addition. Sift together the flour and salt and mix this into the chocolate mixture with the chopped white chocolate. Pour the batter into the prepared pan and bake in the oven for about 30 minutes.

To prepare the glaze, melt the dark chocolate and butter together and spread over the cake. Melt the white chocolate buttons and using a teaspoon trail 5 lines horizontally across the cake about 1 cm (½ in) apart. With a blunt knife draw vertical lines lightly through the chocolate topping to create a pattern.

Mars Bar and Rice Crispies Slice

These are very popular for parties and no one will know what they are made from if you don't tell them! They will keep for one week if they are not gobbled up sooner!

Makes 20 slices

3 x 65 g (1½ oz) Mars Bars
90 g (3½ oz) butter
75 g (3 oz) Rice Crispies

Topping
200 g (7 oz) plain chocolate
25 g (1 oz) butter

Grease a 28 x 18 cm (11 x 7 in) shallow tin. Melt the Mars Bars and butter in a saucepan, stirring occasionally (don't boil). Stir in the Rice Crispies. Press into the tin and set aside in the fridge to set for about 1 hour. For the topping, put the chocolate and butter in a saucepan and heat gently, stirring occasionally until melted. Spread the topping over the Rice Crispie mixture and when cool, put in the fridge to set. With a sharp knife, cut into 20 bars.

Desserts

Caramelised Almond Ice Cream

This ice cream tastes sensational, is very simple to make and you don't need to use an ice cream machine. As a variation this is also very good using pecans instead of almonds. It goes well with fresh peaches, which can be served hot with some ice cream on the side. Simply wash and stone the peaches, cut in half, and sprinkle with a little brown sugar. Place under a pre-heated grill for a few minutes.

Serves 6

1 x 410 g (14 oz) can of evaporated milk

Caramelised almonds
225 g (8 oz) blanched almonds
225 g (8 oz) soft brown sugar

45 ml (3 tbsp) cold water
150 g (5 oz) caster sugar
300 ml (½ pint) double cream
10 ml (2 tsp) vanilla essence

Chill the can of evaporated milk in the freezer for about 3 hours. For the caramelised almonds, toast the almonds under a pre-heated grill for a few minutes until golden, turning once. Put the sugar into a heavy-bottomed saucepan together with the water and cook, stirring, over a gentle heat until it caramelises. Stir in the almonds and coat with the sticky caramel. Transfer to a baking tray to cool down.

Once cool, place the caramelised almonds in a tea towel, wrap up and crush with a mallet or rolling pin. Whip the frozen milk with the caster sugar until thick. Whip the double cream and mix into the evaporated milk mixture together with the vanilla essence and the crushed almonds. Put into a suitable container and freeze.

Summer Fruit Brulée with Amaretto Biscuits

This is one of my favourite desserts and is particularly good in summer when peaches and berry fruits are in season. You can also make this using other combinations of fruits – but it's important that the fruit should be really ripe and have a good flavour. Fruits that work well are mangoes, grapes, nectarines, strawberries, kiwis, and you could mix in some passion fruit pulp if you like.

Makes 6 portions

150 g (5 oz) blueberries
150 g (5 oz) raspberries
2 ripe juicy peaches, peeled and chopped

50 g (2 oz) amaretto biscuits, crushed
300 ml (½ pint) crème fraîche
1½ tablespoons light muscovado sugar

Mix the fruit together and arrange in an oven-proof dish. Sprinkle the crushed amaretto biscuits on top and pour over the crème fraîche. Set aside in the fridge for at least 1 hour. Sprinkle over the brown sugar and place under a pre-heated grill for a few minutes until golden.

Louise's Apple and Blackberry Pudding

Louise is a good friend of mine who has two children, Olivia and Ben, both of whom are very fussy eaters. This is one of her children's favourite desserts and it's quick and easy to make. Blackberries are rich in vitamin C and my children love them. Here the slightly tart flavour of the fruit blends really well with the almond sponge topping. Serve hot on its own or with custard or vanilla ice cream.

Serves 4

100 g (4 oz) butter
100 g (4 oz) caster sugar
2 eggs
100 g (4 oz) ground almonds

5 ml (1 tsp) almond essence
450 g (1 lb) cooking apples, peeled and sliced
225 g (8 oz) blackberries, fresh or frozen

Pre-heat the oven to 170°C/325°F/Gas 3. Cream together the butter and sugar and beat in the eggs, ground almonds and almond essence. Mix together the fruit and place in an oven-proof dish. Spread the topping over the fruit and bake in the oven for 45 minutes.

Raspberry and Blueberry Fool

You could also make this using a variety of different fruits or instead use frozen mixed summer berries.

Makes 4 portions

200 g (7 oz) raspberries
100 g (4 oz) blueberries
1 tablespoon rosewater

100 g (4 oz) caster sugar
1 x 250 g (9 oz) tub fromage frais
1 x 200 g (7 oz) tub Greek yoghurt

Keep back about 12 raspberries for decoration. Put the rest of the fruit into a blender with the rosewater and 75 g (3 oz) of the sugar. Blitz until smooth and then press through a sieve into a bowl.

In a separate bowl, beat the fromage frais with the remaining sugar and beat in the yoghurt followed by the raspberry and blueberry purée. Spoon into 4 bowls and top with the reserved raspberries. Serve immediately or chill in the fridge.

Desert Island Pineapple

Here is a very attractive way to serve fresh fruit for a special occasion. (*See photograph, opposite*)

Serves 6

*1 large pineapple
assorted fruit,
such as strawberries, blueberries,*

*raspberries
white grapes*

Choose a large pineapple with attractive-looking leaves. Cut the base flat and peel the pineapple, leaving some peel at the bottom to make a steady base for the tree. With a sharp knife, remove the flesh, leaving the hard core to form the trunk of the tree, but leave some of the flesh around the base.

Place the palm tree on a flat plate and arrange the fresh chunks of pineapple around it together with the assorted fresh fruits and decorate the palm tree with the white grapes – small bunches can be tied to the tree with a length of string.

Strawberry and Lychee Lollies

It's easy to make your own ice lollies using fresh or tinned fruit. You can also make fresh fruit lollies simply by pouring fruit smoothies or pure fruit juice into an ice-lolly mould. This delicious ice lolly is so simple to make but is very popular with my children.

Makes 6 lollies

*1 x 425 g (15 oz) tin lychees in syrup
150 g (5 oz) fresh strawberries, hulled and cut
in half*

Purée the lychees and syrup together with the fresh strawberries. Strain through a sieve. Pour into ice-lolly moulds and freeze.

Auntie Ruthie's Quick and Easy Cheesecake

It will be hard to beat the taste of this delicious cheesecake and it's very quick and simple to prepare. Serve it plain or with the fresh strawberry topping. For best results use a good quality fresh cream cheese.

Serves 6

225 g (7½ oz) digestive biscuits
125 g (4½ oz) butter

600 g (1 lb 5 oz) cream cheese
150 g (5 oz) caster sugar
2 large eggs
5 ml (1 tsp) vanilla essence
600 ml (1 pint) sour cream
2 tablespoons granulated sugar

Strawberry topping
550 g (1¼ lb) strawberries
45 ml (3 tbsp) seedless raspberry jam

Pre-heat the oven to 180°C/350°F/Gas 4. To make the base, crush the digestive biscuits. This can be done by breaking up the biscuits, putting them in a large plastic bag and crushing them with a rolling pin or alternatively break them up in a food processor. Melt the butter and stir the melted butter into the crushed biscuits.

Line the base and grease a 23 cm (9 in) loose-bottomed cake tin and spoon the crumbs over the base, pressing down well (a potato masher is useful for this). In a food processor, beat together the cream cheese, sugar, eggs, vanilla essence and half the sour cream. Pour the cream cheese mixture over the biscuit base and bake in the oven for 25 minutes. Pour over the remaining sour cream mixed with the granulated sugar and then bake for a further 15 minutes.

While the cake is baking in the oven, you can prepare the topping. Spread the raspberry jam in a baking dish and arrange 225 g (8 oz) of halved strawberries on top. Cover with foil and cook at 180°C/350°F/Gas 4 for 20 minutes. Drain the sauce and discard the cooked strawberries. Simmer the sauce in a small saucepan until syrupy. Arrange the remaining strawberries on top of the cake and brush with the syrup.

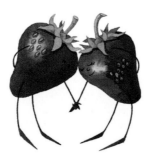

Tiramisu

This popular Italian dessert known as a 'pick me up' is quick and easy to make and is a great way to end a meal. Since this dessert contains raw eggs it should not be eaten by young children.

Makes 6 servings

3 eggs
100 g (4 oz) caster sugar
52.5 ml (3½ tbsp) Marsala wine
400 g (14 oz) Mascarpone cheese

a pinch of salt
250 ml (8 fl oz) strong coffee
24 boudoir biscuits
1 tablespoon cocoa powder

Separate the eggs, put the yolks into a mixing bowl and two of the egg whites into another bowl. Add the sugar to the egg yolks and beat until thick and creamy. Stir in the Marsala and the Mascarpone cheese and mix together with the beaten yolks. Add a pinch of salt to the egg whites and beat until they form stiff peaks. Fold the egg whites into the first mixture until combined. Choose a rectangular dish in which to serve the Tiramisu or prepare individual portions. Pour the coffee into a shallow bowl and dip the boudoir biscuits into the coffee one at a time so that they absorb some of the liquid.

Arrange half the biscuits on the base of the dish, cover with half the Mascarpone mixture, then spoon the remaining Mascarpone mixture on top. Sprinkle the surface with cocoa powder – this is best done using a sieve. Set aside in the fridge for about 4 hours before serving.

Jelly Boats

These jelly boats are one of the most popular party foods that I make. *(See photograph, page 174.)*

Makes 16 boats

4 large oranges, halved
2 x 135 g (4½ oz) packets of jelly, e.g.
raspberry, strawberry, peach, orange, lime

4 sheets rice paper
16 cocktail sticks

With a sharp knife, remove the inside flesh of the oranges and carefully scrape out the membrane, taking care not to make a hole in the skin of the oranges. To make up the jelly, place the cubes in a microwaveable measuring jug, add 3 tablespoons boiling water and heat on full power for 1–1½ minutes. Stir until completely dissolved then make up to 450 ml with cold water. Fill each of the hollow orange halves with jelly right to the top. If you like, you can place them in muffin or bun trays to keep them steady. Refrigerate until set and then trim the orange halves so that the skin of the orange is level with the jelly. Cut the oranges in half again with a sharp knife. Cut triangles out of the rice paper and secure with cocktail sticks to make sails.

Pancakes with Strawberries and Toffee

It's fun for children to make pancakes and you can try to teach them how to toss and catch them in the pan. I love these thin pancakes with a strawberry filling and irresistible warm toffee sauce. They are also good served plain with lemon and sugar or with a little golden syrup. You can make the pancakes in advance and freeze them or store them in the fridge for a couple of days interleaved with greaseproof paper and covered with clingfilm.

Makes 8
pancakes

15 g (½ oz) caster sugar
150 g (5 oz) plain flour
2 eggs
250 ml (8 fl oz) milk
2 tablespoons sunflower oil
125 g (4½ oz) light cream cheese
200 g (7 oz) strawberries, sliced

Toffee sauce
50 g (2 oz) butter
50 g (2 oz) light brown sugar
150 ml (¼ pint) double cream
½ teaspoon vanilla essence

Measure the sugar and flour into a bowl. Make a well in the centre. Add the eggs, then slowly add the milk and mix together until smooth.

Heat the oil in a small omelette pan. Pour a little of the mixture into the pan, tilt to coat the pan and cook for 2–3 minutes. Carefully turn over and cook on the other side, then slide onto a plate while you make the rest. Place a pancake on a board and spread a tablespoon of cream cheese in the centre. Arrange a few slices of strawberries over the cream cheese. Fold two sides into the centre, then fold in half lengthways so you have a rough square shape. Repeat with the remaining pancakes.

To make the toffee sauce, melt the butter in a small pan. Add the sugar and cream and slowly bring to the boil. Remove the pan from the heat and add the vanilla. Pour a little of the sauce over the pancakes.

Evelyn's Lokshen Pudding

This is a favourite pudding that my mother used to make when I was a child. I now make it for my son Nicholas, who loves it just as much as I did – if not more so.

Makes 6 portions

225 g (8 oz) vermicelli (lokshen)
2 eggs
45 ml (3 tbsp) double cream
2 heaped tablespoons caster sugar
2.5 ml (½ tsp) vanilla essence

50 g (2 oz) each raisins and sultanas
1 teaspoon brown sugar
½ teaspoon cinnamon
a generous knob of butter

Pre-heat the oven to 180°C/350°F/Gas 4 and thoroughly butter a fairly shallow dish. Cook the vermicelli in a large pan of lightly salted water according to the instructions on the packet. When cooked, wash well under cold water. Beat the eggs well, add the cream, sugar, vanilla essence, raisins and sultanas. Fold in the lokshen and bake in the prepared dish. Sprinkle with the brown sugar and cinnamon and dot the top with a little butter. Bake in the oven for 35 minutes.

Nectarine, Apple and Raspberry Crumble

A really good crumble bursting with fruit is comfort food at its very best. Other good fruit fillings are rhubarb, gooseberry, blackberry and apple or strawberry and plum. Serve hot with vanilla ice cream or custard.

Makes 5 portions

2 sweet eating apples
25 g (1 oz) butter
2 tablespoons soft brown sugar
2 white nectarines (or you can use peaches)
150 g (6 oz) raspberries
3 tablespoons ground almonds

Topping
150 g (5 oz) plain flour
a generous pinch of salt
100 g (4 oz) cold butter, cut into pieces
75 g (3 oz) demerera sugar
50 g (2 oz) ground almonds

Pre-heat the oven to 200°C/400°F/Gas 6. Peel and core the apples and cut into slices. Melt the butter in a saucepan. Add the sliced apples to the pan, sprinkle with the soft brown sugar and cook for 2 to 3 minutes. Remove from the heat. Peel and core the nectarines and cut into slices. Add these to the cooked apples together with the raspberries. Sprinkle 3 tablespoons of ground almonds into a suitable ovenproof dish (a round dish with a 17 cm/7 inch diameter is ideal). Spoon the fruit into the dish. To make the topping, mix the flour with the salt and demerera sugar. Cut the butter into pieces and rub in with your fingertips until the mixture resembles breadcrumbs. Rub in the ground almonds and cover the fruit with the crumble topping. Sprinkle over a tablespoon of water, which will help to make the topping crispy. Bake in the oven for 30 to 35 minutes or until the topping is lightly golden.

Iced Berries with Hot White Chocolate Sauce

The slightly frozen berries melt into the warm chocolate sauce, giving a delicious contrast.

Makes 4 portions

500 g (1 lb 2 oz) mixed frozen berries e.g. blackberries, blueberries, raspberries, redcurrants

Sauce
142 ml (4½ fl oz) carton double cream
140 g (5 oz) white chocolate

Put the berries in a suitable container and place in the freezer for a couple of hours until semi-frozen. Melt the white chocolate together with the double cream in a heatproof bowl over a pan of simmering water. Don't allow the base of the bowl to come into contact with the water. Stir until the chocolate has melted into the cream. Scatter the frozen fruits on four plates or in shallow bowls, pour over the hot chocolate sauce and serve immediately.

Yvonne's Malva Pudding

Yvonne is a very good friend of mine who lives in Cape Town. I used to teach her daughter to play the harp and whenever I gave concerts Yvonne would present me with a cookbook instead of a bouquet of flowers. She is the most fantastic cook and we used to swap recipes long before I ever thought of writing cookbooks myself.

Makes 8 portions

Sponge pudding
225 g (8 oz) sifted flour
1 egg, lightly beaten
1½ teaspoons bicarbonate of soda
5 ml (1 tsp) vinegar
100 g (4 oz) caster sugar
250 ml (8 fl oz) milk
a pinch of salt
1 heaped tablespoon apricot jam
15 g (½ oz) butter

Sauce
175 g (6 oz) caster sugar
250 ml (8 fl oz) milk
250 ml (8 fl oz) whipping or double cream
25 g (1 oz) butter
5 ml (1 tsp) vanilla essence

Pre-heat the oven to 180°C/350°F/Gas 4 and grease an oven-proof dish that measures approximately 25 x 20 cm (10 x 8 in). Combine the ingredients for the pudding to form a smooth batter. Pour into the prepared dish and bake for 35 minutes or until a knife comes out clean. Combine all the ingredients for the sauce in a pan, stir over a medium heat, bring to boiling point but do not boil. Make several holes in the top of the pudding with a skewer and then pour half the sauce into them and serve. Serve the remaining sauce on the side.

Nicholas's Dream Dessert

My son Nicholas and I concocted this heavenly dessert together. We decided to design a pudding using fresh summer berries, cream and crushed meringue. It was a huge success with the whole family and there was not a scrap left. This is also an easy and fun recipe to make with your child. (*See photograph, opposite.*)

Makes 6 portions

450 g (1 lb) raspberries
3-4 tablespoons icing sugar
175 g (6 oz) strawberries, hulled and cut into quarters

300 ml (½ pint) whipping cream
a few drops vanilla essence
4 ready-made meringues (about 75 g/3 oz)

Put the raspberries into a saucepan and heat gently until they become mushy. Press the raspberries through a sieve and reserve the sauce in a small saucepan. Add the sugar to taste and stir over a low heat until the sugar is dissolved. Stir the remaining raspberries and strawberries into the sauce.

Whip the cream together with the vanilla essence until stiff but not too thick. Break the meringues into pieces and fold these into the whipped cream. Spoon a little of the cream and meringue mixture into each of the glasses, cover with some of the berries and then repeat each layer and top with a sprig of mint or some crushed meringue.

Berried Treasure

You can buy rose water in many supermarkets and it gives this fruit compote a lovely flavour. The pomegranate seeds add a crunchy texture that complements the berry fruits.

Makes 4 portions

2 peaches
20 g (½ oz) butter
2 tablespoons golden caster sugar
1 tablespoon rose water
100 g (4 oz) strawberries

100 g (4 oz) blackberries
100 g (4 oz) blueberries
100 g (4 oz) raspberries
½ pomegranate (optional)

Halve and stone the peaches, and cut each half into four slices. Melt the butter in a heavy-bottomed saucepan and sauté the peaches for 1 minute. Sprinkle with the sugar and cook for 1 minute more. Add the rose water and the strawberries, blackberries and blueberries, and heat for about 1 minute. Remove from the heat and stir in the raspberries and pomegranate seeds.

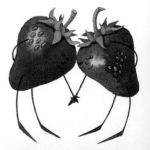

Index

About the Author

Annabel Karmel is the leading author on nutrition and cooking for children and her bestselling books are sold all over the world. Annabel started writing after the loss of her first child, Natasha. Now a mother of three, she is well known for providing advice to millions of parents on what to feed their children, no matter how fussy, as well as getting families to eat a healthier diet without spending hours in the kitchen. Annabel was awarded an MBE in June 2006 by the Queen for her outstanding work in the field of child nutrition.

Her first book *Complete Baby and Toddler Meal Planner*, originally published in 1991, has become the definitive, authoritative guide on feeding babies and children, and has sold several million copies. She is the author of a further 16 books, including *After School Meal Planner*, *Lunchboxes*, *The Fussy Eaters' Recipe Book* and *Top 100 Finger Foods*.

Annabel writes regularly for newspapers and magazines and appears frequently on TV and radio as the UK's top expert on children's nutrition. She has several ranges of healthy ready meals in supermarkets based on her most popular recipes. Her Eat Fussy range of chilled meals for one to four year olds has become very popular in supermarkets across the country. She also has a World Food range for children of four years plus, as well as her own range of sauces and pastas, and an innovative range of equipment and foods called Make it Easy to help parents prepare fresh baby food.

Annabel also produces a range of meals that are now served in all the leading theme parks in the UK, one of the leading nursery groups and in the largest chain of family-based holiday parks. She also writes cookery books for children to learn to cook, and has developed a wide range of quality cooking equipment and cookery kits especially for children.

For more recipes and information visit www.annabelkarmel.com and www.annabelkarmel.tv – an online TV channel offering parents recipes and a step-by-step guide to cooking healthy meals for your child.

Acknowledgments

I want to thank all the children and parents who have been 'guinea pigs' to the successes and failures of my culinary experiments. In particular my mother, Evelyn Etkind, who very seldom uses her own kitchen but has hosted many dinner parties by raiding the contents of my fridge after a day's recipe testing; and my children Nicholas, Lara and Scarlett, who alas now claim that they are too grown-up to be fed purées and have eaten their way through all the recipes in this book and enjoyed lending a hand in cooking some too.

I would also like to thank Dave King for the cover and the photographs of the Raspberry Ripple Cheesecake, Apple, Honey and Raisin Muffins and Pancakes with Strawberries and Toffee, Amelia Thorpe, Joanna Carreras, Carey Smith, Sarah Lavelle, Emma Callery, Christine Carter, Alison Shackleton, Daniel Pangbourne, Harry Ormesher, Val Barrett, Tessa Evelegh, David Karmel, Jacqui Morley, Marina Magpoc, Letty Catada, Nadine Wickenden and Jane Hamilton.

Healthy recipes specially developed for children from Annabel Karmel …

I think it is very important to introduce children to a wide variety of tastes and flavours early on. I have created a range of delicious chilled meals based on favourite recipes from the world, including **Mild Chicken Tikka Masala and Rice** and **Chicken and Vegetable Noodles,** available from supermarkets. Tried and tested, and loved by children, they taste so delicious you'll want to eat them yourself!

Children love to cook too …

And cooking is one of the most important life skills that a child can learn. Encourage your child to cook with one of my kids' baking sets – this exciting 12-piece Princess Baking Set will make a perfect gift.

Getting children to cook is a great way to motivate fussy eaters. As well as learning basic cooking skills such as kneading, grating and separating eggs, through cooking children learn many other skills, such as maths, reading and writing and science, all without noticing.

Inside each set, there are five recipes and all the utensils you'll need!

Available from all good retailers.

Make delicious meals with my tasty cooking sauces and Dinosaur Pasta Shapes

Choose from **Tomato and Basil Sauce**, **Cherry Tomato and Mascarpone Cheese Sauce**, **Tomato and Sweet Potato in Moroccan Style Sauce** and a **Mild Fruit Curry Sauce**. Contribute to your child's five a day; simply mix with Annabel Karmel Dinosaur Pasta, cooked meat, chicken, fish, veg or rice. Alternatively, use a recipe in this book. Available from supermarkets.

Visit my website www.annabelkarmel.com for more recipes, and www.annabelkarmel.tv for cooking videos

Annabel Karmel